The Poser

(Yes...... you are one too!)

Ken Jones

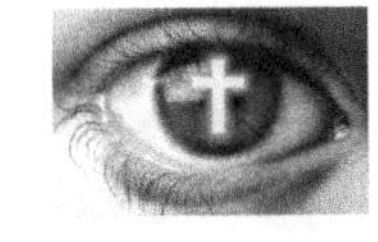

Open Eyes Publishing

Table of Contents

<u>Dedication</u>

This book is dedicated to our Lord and Savior Jesus Christ. The perfect example of how we should live our lives, and the only person to ever walk this earth who never lived the life of a poser.

"Do not conform to the pattern of this world, but be transformed by the renewing of your mind. Then you will be able to test and approve what God's will is—his good, pleasing and perfect will." Romans 12:2

Introduction

The concepts and objectives for this book began taking shape in my mind just over a year ago. And while the overall intention and goal was very clear to me, the minuscule thoughts popping into my head every now and then which would eventually fill the pages were still scattered and disorganized at best. As often happens with writers, a single thought, incident, or experience we stumble upon in our daily routine can suddenly provide the missing link that ties together all the scattered pieces, making the whole picture instantly clear. It is like the proverbial light switch being flicked on in our minds, and it is in this moment that we feel we could sit down and write the entire book effortlessly, without pause.

That moment for me, and this book, came yesterday. The moment, or experience, was a conversation that I was having with a good friend, whom I have known for several years, and whom I assumed that I knew pretty well. That conversation, or at least several of the comments made during that conversation, made me question how well I really knew my friend. And as I continued to ponder my perceptions of him and our friendship late into that night – it shockingly hit me like the cold winds of an Arctic blast. It was not just my friend who possessed these attributes – It was all of us! This is each and every one of us in the world that we live in today! This is who we are, or should I say who we have become, or allowed ourselves to become.

The conversation with my friend on that day was our usual chit-chat; a seemingly light discussion about a specific thought, topic, or idea, accompanied by our own individual thoughts on the matter. However, with this friend, most conversations are short lived, and they rarely have much depth to them. This is mostly because this friend shows outward behaviors typical of someone with ADD, or Attention Deficit Disorder. Any conversation entered in to with this friend frequently and suddenly changes as he jumps from one topic to another. And any response by the opposing individual is always cut short with his rebuttal and counter-response which inevitably strays off topic as well. I am well aware that there may be, and likely is, many other issues or causes for this type of behavior from my friend. However, I am not a psychologist, and the objective of this book is not to analyze or highlight any issues that he may or may not have.

The conversation that we were having took place as we were just about to tee off for a round of golf. My friend and I both claim to be Christians, and both claim to hold our faith in Christ as our number one priority.

Over the years, we've gotten to know each other well enough that we are able to be completely open and honest, knowing the other will be supportive—even when calling out each other's BS and holding one another accountable. The only problem with this understanding is that the one being called out for the errs is not always willing to admit that they were in the wrong to begin with. Many times, when confronted with an opposing view of what is acceptable, that person fails to see the rational for the opposing view and holds firm to their dogmatic beliefs and views, with an unwillingness to even consider that a different view is possible. Dogmatism, the stubborn or intolerant adherence to one's opinions or prejudices, is one of the greatest hindrances to our existence and to realizing our true and full potential.

This was the case during our conversation, following a comment that my friend had made. At this point, I do not recall exactly how we came to that revealing moment in our conversation. The moment where my friend made one simple statement - *"I always adapt to the people around me."*

The comment was unexpected and stopped me in my tracks. I cocked my head back in disbelief and said *"What?"* I was utterly shocked by the statement that he made. He then repeated it again - *"I always adapt to the people around me."* I then quickly asked him - *"Why? Is that what Jesus would do? Did Jesus adapt and change to be like the people He was around just so they would like Him or accept Him?"*

My friend quickly assumed his typical defensive posture and firmly stated that his actions were not of a sinful nature. He said that he did this to get close to people, to know them better, and to build a relationship with them in hopes of being able to share the Gospel with them.

I then asked my friend one more simple question - *"Who created you?"* His response was just as I would have expected when he admitted that he had been created by God. I then reminded him that God is perfect in everything that He does, and that God created each and every one of us just the way we are, for His glory, and not so that we could become like someone else. I went on to state that any attempt at trying to be anything other than our true selves was dishonoring God and was blasphemy, or in a sense saying to God that we have a better way of doing things and getting through life.

My friend refused to even consider the possibilities of my viewpoints and stood firm in his beliefs stating that I was wrong and did not know what I was talking about. Within minutes I began to realize that any further discussion on the matter would only create a divide and harsh feelings, so without much difficulty I changed the topic of our conversation. The thoughts of my friend's understanding troubled me all day however, as I could not comprehend how someone that claimed to be a Godly man and a Christian could hold such a view and perception. And as I allowed my mind to search for a logical justification well into the night, even contemplating the possibility that I could be wrong in my perspective of the matter, that proverbial light switch came on filling my head with the direction for this book.

This scene of events, this understanding and belief, this viewpoint and perspective – This is not just my friend, this is who we all are. Each and every one of us, to some extent at least. We are all posers! We are all something other than what God created and intended us to be. We are all trying to gain the attentions, respect, admiration, support, and affirmation of something or someone else. And in an effort to do so – we change who we truly are, to adapt, so that we may become someone or something that we perceive to be more desirable and worthy.

The most shocking part, just as was the case with my friend, is that many of us have been playing this role as the poser for so long that we even have ourselves convinced that this is who we truly are. And since this fake persona is who we believe we truly are, we are unwilling to acknowledge or accept any possibility that the life we are living is not that of our true selves.

We have long since forgotten who that person was – The person that we once were – That person who we were created and intended to be!

Chapter 1

A Better Life

"He becomes an echo of someone else's music, an actor of a part that has not been written for him."[1]
Oscar Wilde

It is probably not the best idea for an author to risk offending their potential readers in the very first chapter of a book, let alone the title. Sorry to say, but it's true – you are a poser! You've been one your whole life. The reality of the matter is that you have been entrenched in the life of a poser for so long that it is nearly impossible for you to see and accept on your own.

I suppose this already gives you a bit of insight into who I am. I have a tendency to speak my mind. Most people nowadays would say that I don't have a filter. Being straightforward and to the point, I'm not one to sugarcoat my words. Sometimes this can be a good thing, while others it may come across as harsh or cruel. My wife will often catch me, after the fact, suggesting that my delivery could have been a little more delicate. Nonetheless, my intentions are always good and never meaning to cause offense.

The good news, however, is that you're not very good at it. Everyone else can clearly see that you're not real. The only reason that this life seems sincere to you is that this is the image that you want to see. It gives you another option and something different than what you are truly running and hiding from. Oops! There I go again. That was meant to be a compliment, and not offensive.

But yes, a poser you are. And there is most definitely something buried away, deep inside of you, that drove you into the life of a poser. If you're able to set the ego and pride aside for a bit, I will not only prove it to you but also show you the way out of that life and how to get back to the person that you were truly created to be.

So how might I, a common everyday man with an average education, be qualified and found credible in the writing of a book on societal tendencies and human behavior? In all fairness and transparency, I am not a psychologist, I am not a psychiatrist, and I have no doctorate degree of any kind. Honestly, I couldn't stand school. I ended up dropping out during my junior year of high school as I believed I had a better way to reinvent the wheel.

However, I do have something that not one of the major Colleges or Universities could ever teach you – I have experience. Real world experience in living the life of a poser and perfecting the skills required of that life. Skills which enabled me to rise from a poverty stricken, morally bankrupt childhood to a successful life where I was now considered to be in the top 2% per annual income.

During a weekly podcast for his company, which was branded using the title of the book that he wrote, *Wild at Heart*[2] - Best-selling author and counselor John Eldredge gave the following advice to those who may venture into writing - *"Do not write about anything that you have not lived, for then it is only theory."*[3]

I lived this life, that of a poser, for more than forty years. I had mastered the ability to adapt and become something and someone other than my true self. I had spent my entire life attempting to portray myself as something other than who I truly was. And I had become pretty good at it along the way, all while continuing to modify, adjust, and adapt to the people and situations that surrounded me. One can only adapt and change successfully by studiously observing that which they are trying to assimilate. It is through these observations that I learned the true character, tendencies, and faults of mankind which are shared and inherent among every one of us.

My childhood was less than desirable and lacked everything that a young boy needs to make the transition into the real world and become a man of his own. My father left my mother and four young children before I reached the age of ten. My mother was then left to raise four kids on her own, which meant working multiple jobs and never being around for the kids that she chose to bring into this world. With the more seasoned perspective that I have now, I cannot fault her. She had a very difficult choice to make, and I cannot say that I would have done any better if I had been in her shoes, at that place and time. She chose to do what she had to do in order to survive.

My father left my mother to chase after another woman, just as he did when he chased after my mother. My father lived the 'self-life'. It was all about him and what served his interests and desires. Obviously, children, or the future well-being of those children were not one of those desires. Any interaction that I had with my father over the next twenty years, which was limited at best, was superficial and only for show.

For me, this meant that my transition into the real world came at about the age of twelve, with no guidance, no role model, and no adult or manly figure in my life to teach me or train me on even the most basic fundamentals of life.

So how did I learn these much-needed essentials to get by in life? I observed other people and tried to do what they were doing. I studied, watched, and learned what others would do – and then incorporated those things into my life, to do them just as I had seen someone else do them.

Now one might say that this way of learning is harmless, and that it is used quite frequently in our day and age. Nowadays, when we don't know how to do something, it is common practice to pull out your smart phone – and go to 'YouTube University'. Within minutes we can find a short video clip of someone else showing us how to do just about anything. We also have a common practice called 'on the job training', where one is paired with an experienced worker allowing them to learn the needed skills by watching or observing the one who is experienced.

While each of these methods has their own benefits to some extent, they too can be harmful in many ways which we won't delve in to right now. However, both of these methods, as well as the methods which I learned to perfect throughout my life all have one major fault:

The information taken in or perceived by the observer, and to what depth it is applied, is directly related to and limited by the understanding and knowledge of the observer.

To succeed at anything, whether it be life, a new job, or a simple task, we must first have at least a basic understanding of certain fundamentals that relate to that task. And for me, I had no understanding of even the most basic fundamentals of life. My first book, *I Don't Have A Clue How To Live This Life*[4], details my entire life including my childhood years and the specific scenarios which caused me to adapt in ways that I was not even aware of at the time.

As we move forward through the book, it is important to note and remember that I, just as with anyone else living the life of the poser, did not intentionally set out with the desire to become something or someone else. For me, it was an act of survival. The transformation that came about was the result of what I perceived as the only way to get by, and to be accepted by others and this world that we live in. The poser then became who I was, my way of life, even causing me to become oblivious to the fact that I was constantly changing and growing further and further away from my true self.

There are countless reasons why we allow ourselves to change and be changed. And there are just as many causes and actions that push us in this direction as well. Each of us will most certainly have a different cause and reason. Nonetheless, each and every one of us eventually arrives in the life of the poser. And for those who may find this hard to accept, I would suggest that you go back and read the last paragraph, specifically the last sentence, and the part about being oblivious.

If you can allow yourself to open your mind and your heart, setting aside all of the preconceived views that are forced upon us by the world which we live in, we will take a deep dive into the life and role of the Poser. We will learn everything about the poser, from the early stages of this change to the full-blown poser who is no longer capable of remembering the person who they once were - as well as what we can do moving forward to stop being the poser, or someone other than who we truly were created to be.

For more than forty years I lived the life of the poser, completely unaware that not only was I allowing myself to be changed, but that I was altering myself to fit in and adapt as well, just as each and every one of us do every single day. There is a better life my friends, the life that you and I were originally intended to live out, and a life that is fully ours and there for the taking once again!

Let's go get it back!

"For we are God's handiwork, created in Christ Jesus to do good works, which God prepared in advance for us to do."

Ephesians 2:10

Chapter 2

Who Are We?

"It is because we are all impostors that we endure each other. The man who does not consent to lie will see the earth shrink under his feet: we are biologically obliged to the false" [1]
Emile M. Cioran

If we are being honest with ourselves, I think most of us would admit that we don't have a great fondness for other people these days. Especially in this post-Covid era. It seems like the global pandemic, in some ways, has entitled people to be more self-centered, often showing little to no regard or consideration for others.

Common sense no longer exists and any sense that one may have has now been created by their individual perspective, simply for the purpose of furthering their own agenda or acquiring their own desires. Rarely does anyone show care for another anymore, and we are quick to dispose of even the closest people in our lives when that relationship suddenly becomes difficult or the benefits no longer seem to be immediate or gratifying.

The harsh reality is that more often than not, other people just plain suck! C'mon.... You know you've said it too. Or at the very least, thought so. We all have. We all find it harder and harder to interact and deal with other people every single day. And we then find that it consumes us as we spend the better part of our day complaining about it and about others as well.

I'm not really the person I appear to be, and neither are you.
Let's be honest – We're both just putting on an act, aren't we?

The process likely takes hold early in your day. The simple drive to work clearly reveals that anyone else on the road would not give a second thought to running you into a ditch just so there would be one less car to deal with. The clown that cuts you off because he wasn't paying attention and is now about to miss his exit. The bozo who never allows anyone to pass him, simply because being in front of you makes him feel superior and as if he is better than you. And we must not forget the genius that gets onto the interstate and quickly darts all the way over to the left lane, only to drive 5mph under the speed limit, as if he were the only car on the road.

Then you arrive at work, and everyone seems different today. The people that were pleasant and cheerful yesterday now have a completely different demeanor. Hmmmm, it must be me. What is it that I have done to offend them? Do my clothes not match today? Is something wrong with my hair? Do I smell funny? We can't really put a finger on it, so we write them off as being a jerk.

We eventually head back home, fighting those same morons in traffic that we did on the way to work, only to spend our evening in something that feels more like a jail cell than the refuge that it was meant to be. Our tolerance level for others was exceeded hours ago, so we just sink into the couch and stare at the TV all night hoping that no one expects or needs our attention.

There is no peace. There is no joy. No happiness or relaxation. This is our life – day after day. What once was a passion filled person with hopes, dreams, and desires has now become a worn out, beaten down, pile of sludge who just wants to be left alone. Our whole existence has boiled down to simply trying to survive. That person who once strived to get ahead, at least for some period of time, and now just tries to keep up. This is what our lives have become as we struggle to grab whatever we can for ourselves, while we can. We are all afraid. Afraid of falling behind and being left behind.

We have turned our lives into a competition. And in doing so, we either find ourselves in a place that we will do whatever it takes to win or we run and hide from everything so as not to be seen as the loser. Whichever path we choose, each and every one of us does whatever we can to simply survive, all the while sacrificing any morals or values that we once may have clung too.

Modern day scientists believe that we are born with this survival instinct. And while to some extent, on a more primary level, we may be - the survival instinct that we are referring to now is one that is learned through the environment which we are a part of throughout our lives. It is what we are taught. It is what we are programmed to believe and accept as the way to make our lives run more effectively and efficiently.

This cultivated survival instinct is triggered within us by a perceived threat. Something or someone that we envision as being harmful to the ways in which we see our lives playing out, and detrimental to the fundamental beliefs which we have built our lives around. Our flawed perception then leads us to believe that if someone or something which we perceive as harmful were to succeed, then the opposite must be true for us, and we would lose. It is a law that is instilled in us from early on – There can be only one winner! Once again – We are all afraid of falling behind and being left behind. And that fear is what drives most all of us in much of everything that we do.

This, however, is not who we truly are as a person. It is simply what we have become and what we have allowed ourselves to become in an effort to survive and be accepted. This is not who we were created to be. At some point in our lives, each and every one of us were greatly deceived. And those deceptions continue to bombard us with such frequency throughout our lives that we have come to accept them as the norm. This is life. This is the way that things are. Or so we allow ourselves to believe.

Why is it that we have become so consumed with the thoughts, emotions, and the actions of other people? Why is it so important to us what others may think? More importantly – why do we allow these other people to control our thoughts, emotions, and actions?

Believe It or Not

Many of us will likely struggle to accept the fact, or even come to realize, that each and every one of us is a poser. Yes, you are one as well! All of us, at least to some degree, are inauthentic. We are fake, we are phony, we are counterfeit, we are a fraud. We are merely an imitation or variation of someone or something other than the person whom we were created to be. Much like the chameleon, we are constantly changing to blend in with our surroundings, simply for our survival.

In some of us, this disguise is easily detectable as it rarely comes to surface, and then only during specific moments, occasions, or surroundings which we may find ourselves in. The unmistakable contrast in the identity and personality of this poser makes it clearly evident through the change which occurs. This type of poser emerges more so out of an immediate need or desire. It is as if the individual possesses two completely different personalities, and has the ability to call upon either at will. This type of person is what I refer to as the Periodic Poser. Being a poser is not what they have fully become, or for the most part, who they truly are. However, for one reason or another, they have created a completely different person within themselves; a person that is contrary to their true being.

The vast majority of posers, however, are the true phonies and frauds. These are the Full-Blown Posers and include those who are on the path to becoming one as well. Their entire being has been built around becoming something and someone different than who they were created to be, and who they once were. More than likely, their transformation began at a young age. And just like the Periodic Poser, their beginning into the life of a poser was deemed to be necessary due to a wound or injury they once received, and their ensuing perspective of that wound or injury.

The Full-Blown Poser creates an entirely new existence of who they are, what they believe, and how they view all things. It is not long before the Full-Blown Poser completely forgets the person that they once were, as for one reason or another they have wholeheartedly committed to becoming someone other than the person they were created to be. It is also not long before the Full-Blown Poser fully believes that this new identity is the person that they have always been, and the person that they were created to be. Out of self-preservation and protection, they will also refuse to accept any possibility that they have altered or changed in any way.

While there are many other variations to the poser, and even more causes for one becoming a poser, the Periodic Poser and the Full-Blown Poser are the two most common in our world today. Our discussions will stay with these two subtypes throughout the remainder of the book. We will also unravel how it is not only possible, but almost a certainty, that you too have become a poser.

My intentions through this book are not to point fingers at anyone, or to bring shame in any way. If you are finding yourself already offended in just the first several pages of the book.... Stop, for just a minute, and hit pause! Take a few deep breathes. Then remember – this book is to help you and others realize the trap of deception that all of us have been living in.

This book is to help you and others find the way back to that person who is the real you. To help you believe that the person who you once were is actually more than good enough, and to show you that there truly is a much better and greater life out there just waiting for you – which is still there for you – and is still yours for the taking!

Keep this in mind as well – I was the King of Posers. I had mastered the art of being a poser. My entire existence had become a hoax which was built around the lies and deceptions that I perceived as reality. I too once believed that I had to become something different, as the true me was not good enough. And that my friends, is not something that I am proud of. I had lived this life for the better part of my existence. I know all too well the struggles, the pains, and the frustrations that come with this life. I know that feeling of hopelessness as we are never able to find that which we are searching for.

My greatest reason for writing this book is that I know exactly where life as a poser leads us – a dark, desolate, barren place that I pray no one ever has to experience again. Sadly, I am well aware that many of you, even after reading this book, will sooner than later find yourselves in that exact place as you discard the information within as rubbish. This too is not you; it is the enemy that we face, the one who wants so badly to keep all of us in that miserable existence.

Understand that I am no better than you, and that I had to come to grips with these same hard truths at one point as well. Purely through the grace of God, my eyes were opened, and I was able to see the lie that I had been living. I no longer live that counterfeit life. I now live the life that God had always intended for me to live – my life, being me! Being happy and being free! And through this book, that is what I desire for you as well.

> When we are dealing with something about which we are ignorant, we must be slow to criticize just because we are uncomfortable with some of the things that accompany what we don't know. Ignorance is not grounds for rejection.

Definition

The word *POSER* is a noun and is derived from the word pose. The word Pose as defined in the Merriam-Webster dictionary, when used as a noun, has a meaning of:

- a sustained posture, especially - one assumed for artistic effect

- an attitude, role, or characteristic assumed for effect

The intransitive (not having or containing a direct object) verb pose means:

-to assume a posture or attitude usually for artistic purposes

- to affect an attitude or character usually to deceive or impress

The *Poser* (noun) is a person who has taken on a pose (a form of actions, an image, characteristics, qualities, or personality other than their true being) to assume a posture, attitude, or image of something other than what they truly are – for artistic purposes, most always to deceive or impress others.

The poser within us is the life each of us has chosen to live, yet none of us are willing to admit to.

One of the first questions which comes to mind is – Why? Why would someone want or need to assume a posture, attitude, or image of something other than who and what they truly are and were created to be? As the definition further explains, we do this most often in an attempt to deceive or impress others.

That, albeit is the truncated answer. Fully grasping the reasoning and intentions behind the *Why* is far more complex than it may seem, as we'll soon discover in the chapters ahead.

In 1978, two Psychologists created a label for those who possess these traits. Dr. Pauline Clance and Dr. Suzanne Imes first coined the term *"impostor syndrome"* when they published *"The Impostor Phenomenon in High Achieving Women: Dynamics and Therapeutic Intervention"*.[2]

Clance and Imes defined impostor phenomenon as "an internal experience of intellectual phoniness". In 1985, Clance published a book on the topic, and the phenomenon became widely known. Initially, Clance identified the syndrome with high-achieving professional women, but later studies found that it was widespread in both men and women and in many professional settings.

Modern day Psychologists have since modified the term, now referring to it as *impostor phenomenon*, as the word *syndrome* can be offensive and implies an underlying disease or disorder. I find it rather ironic that the professionals who use this label to describe the characteristics and tendencies of others who change and adapt so that they may fit in and be accepted have also modified their methods and terminology so that it may be more acceptable and pleasing to others. Once again – all of us do it!

However, it should be noted that impostor syndrome is not a recognized psychiatric disorder and is not featured in the American Psychiatric Association's Diagnostic and Statistical Manual nor is it listed as a diagnosis in the International Classification of Diseases.[3]

According to Clance, impostor syndrome is a psychological experience of intellectual and professional fraudulence. Or, for those of us without a PhD – the subjective experience of perceived self-doubt in one's abilities and accomplishments compared with others, despite evidence to suggest the contrary.

Those who have this syndrome or phenomenon may doubt their skills, talents, or accomplishments. They may have a persistent internalized fear of being exposed as a fraud. Despite external evidence of their competence, those experiencing this phenomenon do not believe they deserve their success or luck. They may perceive themselves to be deceiving others because they feel as if they are not as intelligent as they outwardly portray themselves to be.

Impostor phenomenon is studied as a reaction to particular stimuli and events. It is an experience that a person has, and how they perceive that experience, not a mental disorder. Impostor phenomenon is not recognized in the DSM or ICD[3], although both of these classification systems recognize low self-esteem and a sense of failure as associated symptoms of depression. Although impostor phenomenon is not a pathological condition, it is a distorted system of belief about oneself that can have a powerful negative impact on a person's valuation of their own worth.

People with impostor syndrome have a much greater chance to suffer from depression and anxiety. They are also more likely to experience low self-esteem, somatic symptoms and social dysfunctions.

While the tendencies of the impostor, or poser, will vary from individual to individual; they all have at least a few common traits which they share.

Denial

A thought or attitude which may have quickly surfaced for you by now is one of denial. As you scan these pages, taking in the details and reading the definition, you silently tell yourself -*"This is not me! I am not fake or phony in any way. I am my true self, and the author is simply talking about other people.*

Defensiveness is one of the key traits for the poser or impostor. A poser, or impostor, is basically living a lie, and a liar is always trying to cover their tracks. Becoming defensive about their thoughts, words, actions, or decisions is par for the course. They are quick to make excuses, point fingers, and lay blame in order to save themselves from having to accept the fact that they are counterfeit.

Denial is a cognitive process which involves refusing to acknowledge or accept reality, even when that reality presents itself with objective facts, often serving as a defense mechanism against painful feelings or stress. This can manifest in the human mind where one consciously or subconsciously avoids or minimizes certain aspects of reality. Denial also involves an attitude of resistance or our refusal to face the truth, which then affects and alters our behavior and interactions.

Therefore, the simple thought or attitude of denial which you may have just experienced might mean that we are on to something here. Each of us carry wounds, scars, and painful memories acquired from our past. It is through these traumatic events that we are most always led to modify, adapt, alter and change the person that we once were.

Adaptation

W. Clement Stone provided us with the well-known quote *"We are all a product of our own environment."*[4]

So, what exactly does this mean, and how does it relate to our everyday lives? The foundation of the quote implies that we are all inherently different, and that each of us will adapt or conform to become a by-product or the derivative of our surroundings. This innate quality, more or less, is a survival instinct that each of us have. We adapt to our surroundings and environment in an attempt to fit in and be accepted as part of what we perceive to be the more dominant and authoritative group that exists in our lives at the time. Simply put – we modify who we truly are to become more like the others around us so that we may be liked and more desirable, so that we may fit in and be accepted.

This change, alteration, or adaptation is commenced for many reasons which we will detail in later chapters. However, the primary trigger that drives us to this change is not specifically an action, occurrence, or that one traumatic event; but the way in which we perceive that action or occurrence and how we then allow it to affect our view of reality.

Whoa!!! That may be one of the most significant statements in the book, and one worth retaining. You should probably get your highlighter out, mark it, and say it again.

The primary trigger that drives us to this change is not specifically an action, occurrence, or that one traumatic event; but the way in which we perceive that action or occurrence and how we then allow it to affect our view of reality.

Grab a bookmark and place it onto the top of the previous page as this is one of the key takeaways from the book which we will build upon in later chapters. I often use the little yellow sticky 'post it' notes, writing a comment on the upper portion that I leave sticking out, so with one quick glance I can see the topic of importance. For this note I would write out: *How we see things affects our reality.*

The adaptation of the poser begins early in our lives, at a very young age, most often due to a trauma or wound that someone else has inflicted upon us. We then allow ourselves to create a new version of who we are out of self-protection, or a lack of self-confidence or belief, as we perceive that the old version of us is just not good enough, strong enough, or just plain not-enough.

The modifications do not stop there, however. We continue to make these changes throughout our entire lives, continually attempting to adapt to whatever environment we may be in at the time and constantly growing further and further away from the person whom we were created to be.

This, of course, is only a simplified explanation of what the poser is. It would take countless books to fully illustrate the reasoning, characteristics, types and tendencies of the poser. In the limited time and space that we have in this book, however, we will hopefully scratch the surface, inspiring you to question your life, as well as who and what you have become. For those who do commit to fully returning to the person that you once were, you might even come to realize the exact moment or event in your life that led you to become a poser.

In the following chapters we will find out how all of us have come to be posers, what has caused us to become something different than who we were created to be, and how we can find our way back to the person that we once were.

There is a much greater and happier existence awaiting each and every one of us. To obtain it, all we need to do is find our way back and then learn to embrace that person who we once were – that person whom we did not think was enough.

"So God created mankind in his own image, in the image of God he created them; male and female he created them." Genesis 1:27

Chapter 3

In The Beginning

To fully understand the life of a poser, we must first possess a few fundamental beliefs of this life and the world which we live in. These beliefs are paramount to our understanding of all things. Without them, nothing really seems to make sense—just like the life we've been living.

First and foremost – we must wholeheartedly believe that God does exist, that God is the creator of all things, and that in His sovereignty God does have complete control over all things. A common stumbling block for many of us in this belief is the word control. We place an intense fixation on that one word alone, or on the phrase 'control over all things', and instinctively assume a defensive posture. We want control over our lives and we surely don't want anyone else telling us what to do or how to live the life that is ours. We assume that if we 'give in' to this belief we are essentially relinquishing our freedom and allowing someone else to determine our fate and outcome. However, nothing could be further from the truth. This way of thinking is just one of the many great deceptions that we have been led to accept as our reality. Hopefully, as you read on, this will become more evident, and you will begin to understand the true character and intentions of our loving God.

Another misconception that the world has taught us is that if God does have control over all things – He is the cause of all things that happen. Eventually, something bad happens in someone's life, and since God controls all things, they quickly blame God and label Him as cruel and one who does not care. In reality, control and causation are not related. Personally, I would like to think that I have control over my children and my family. However, that control does not mean that I cause them to do everything that they do. What we will learn more of as we move forward is that there is a whole lot more going on in our world and our lives than we are able to comprehend, and while God may allow certain things to happen, He is not always the one causing them to happen.

Any refusal to accept this belief, that God does exist, only further validates the truth of the next two beliefs, and the fact that each of us is held in bondage by Satan, some much longer than others.

It is a necessity that we also believe in Jesus Christ, and that He is the son of the one true living God. The Bible clearly foretells the birth of Christ in the Old Testament and undeniably declares Him as the Son of God and our Savior, to be sacrificed for the redemption of our sins. The Bible also makes it clear that our only path to having a relationship with God is through Jesus Christ himself.

Jesus makes the point irrefutable in John 14:6 when He says: *"I am the way and the truth and the life. No one comes to the Father except through me."*

Second – we must accept and believe that Satan exists as well, and that Satan is actively involved in our everyday lives regardless of whether we choose to acknowledge him or not. Once again, a refusal to accept this belief only confirms the veil of darkness that Satan himself has cast over us, to keep us from seeing and knowing the truth. Therefore, the cognitive process of our denial, most always due to something being painful or uncomfortable, lies within our internal refusal to accept reality - or - The world has trained us to believe that if we do talk about Satan, or acknowledge that he does exist, that we will be seen as a lunatic. The world has made it uncomfortable and therefore not a part of our reality.

"Satan, who is the god of this world, has blinded the minds of those who don't believe. They are unable to see the glorious light of the Good News. They don't understand this message about the glory of Christ, who is the exact likeness of God."
2 Corinthians 4:4 NLT

Finally, we must believe that the Bible is the true Word of God, that it was inspired by God, and that it has just as much relevance to our lives today as it did two thousand years ago.

"All Scripture is God-breathed and is useful for teaching, rebuking, correcting and training in righteousness," 2 Tim 3:16

[20]*"Above all, you must understand that no prophecy of Scripture came about by the prophet's own interpretation of things.* [21]*For prophecy never had its origin in the human will, but prophets, though human, spoke from God as they were carried along by the Holy Spirit."* 2 Peter 1:20-21

Any rejection of the Bible or its validity that we may possess comes solely from Satan with the intent purpose of keeping us from knowing God, knowing the truths, and knowing who it is that we were truly created to be.

In 1 John Chapter 4, the Apostle John states: [1]*"Dear friends, do not believe every spirit, but test the spirits to see whether they are from God..... * [3]*but every spirit that does not acknowledge Jesus is not from God. This is the spirit of the antichrist...."*

John makes it clear that there are spirits of good, being from God, and spirits of evil, being from Satan or the antichrist, and that both are very much present and active in our world today.

We have a reluctance to accept these statements as fact and reality simply because we haven't been given the full story. There has been a monumental shift in society over the past few centuries, as well as in our churches. This new paradigm has become a disease which is now known as *the disease to please*. And much like the poser, all of us have this disease and use it to avoid displeasing other people, or to avoid the discomfort we may incur when standing up for what we believe in.

Over the past few hundred years, society and our churches have continued to alter the image, understanding, message and character of God in an attempt to be more appealing – or, to create a version of the story that makes others feel good about themselves. Nowadays, in just about any church or religious facility, what you will see and hear is the 'feel-good gospel'. The true story of our lives and existence has been edited countless times with many parts being redacted and omitted. The true story, our true story, is not the story that we have been told and certainly not the true image and representation of who God and Jesus are.

I am in no way implying that the message you may hear in every church is a lie, even though there are many that are preaching anything but the truth. What I am stating is that most churches nowadays are only telling you half of the story. What you will see and hear is a version of God, Jesus, and our history which has been altered and made to look pretty and make you feel good – so that you are comfortable and will keep coming back. And we have to be honest with ourselves - half of the story is not going to get you or me back to the person we were created to be. If we truly want to know who God and Jesus are, and how they affect our lives and our future, we need the whole story. We need the truth.

If we cannot allow ourselves to accept these truths as an essential part of our core beliefs, there is nothing to be gained by reading any further. These three points are the underlying and foundational truths to life, to our world, and to everything that exists. If we are unable to accept and believe these points as being true, everything that we have built our lives upon and around is simply a lie.

It is also not possible for us to leave the poser life behind without accepting these beliefs. One of the primary reasons for our venture into the life of a poser was our lack of belief and commitment to these truths. As we will soon discover, it was the lies and deceptions that we chose to accept and believe as reality which led us astray to begin with.

Separation

With these beliefs, and the reading of the Bible, we become aware that prior to the beginning of our world, there was only the Heavenly realm. A perfect existence of God, angels, and spiritual beings. There was no sin, no hate, no anger, no diseases, no lies, and no death. Everything in existence was perfect, made by the perfect hand of God, and created to honor and glorify God.

The two most powerful angels, known as Archangels, were Micheal and Samael. One day, Samael decided that he wanted to be like God, having all power and control. He then proceeded to deceive many other angels with the lie that they too could be all powerful, and he began a great war in the Heavens attempting to overthrow God and take control.

Some of you may be a bit puzzled, and you may be asking yourself – *If God had made everything perfect, and there was no sin in Heaven, how was it possible that one of the angels was able to become rebellious?*

When God created the angels, He gave them free will, just as He has done with us. This free will is the freedom for one to choose and make choices on their own. God wanted the angels, and us, to seek Him out and choose Him out of our own love and desire for Him - Just as we would do in any other relationship or desire which we may have. When we truly love and desire something, we chase after it and focus all of our attentions on it.

God could have created us in a way where we were unwillingly forced to love Him, but that would make God a dictator or tyrant and would then not be true love. God gave us the freedom of choice, free will, and God will always give us over to what we seek and desire. God even loves and cares for those who do not believe in Him, giving them what they seek and desire as well.

There are countless reasons why people do not believe in God. All of which originate from the lies and deceptions that we allow ourselves to believe and accept as an alternative reality. One significant struggle that many retain is that of authority – people are not willing to believe in a God that requires them to submit themselves to His authority. We like power and control, and we like to think that we have control over all aspects of our lives, including all others in our lives. Those with this struggle hold the view that if they do believe in God they would then be placing someone or something higher than themselves. It's the self-life, and a bit narcissistic to say the least. None the less, they would then be required to submit to someone or something else, giving up that sense of having control.

Control is an interesting topic. We like to think that it gives us power and freedom. Control, however, is one of the greatest deceptions of all time. It actually robs us of any true power or freedom. And any control that we do think we have – well, that was created out of fear. Yes, that's right. Created out of a fear that we had and still may have. It is the result of one of the wounds we received in our past, which we will discuss more in Chapter 4.

Either way, the person with this perspective believes that by choosing God they will lose any hope of ever getting the things they want and desire. They believe that God will make their lives boring and sterile. Again, nothing could be further from the truth. God wants to give each and every one of us the fullest life and all of our desires. And the reality of the matter is that whether we choose God or not, He does give us whatever we desire.

When one's heart is so hardened against God, and full of nothing but a life of sin, God gives them over to this life which they so fully desire. Furthermore, while it is true that God does rule over all things, and does have absolute power, God desires for us to reign and rule with Him.

Back to our story – Samael and his deceived angels were badly beaten in that war and then cast out of Heaven. Not long after, God created our world, and mankind. And yet again, everything that He created was perfect. God created the first human beings, Adam and Eve, who were perfect and sinless and were to live forever in a perfect world which would provide for their every need.

Samael, now known as Satan, still had it out for God. And since he was unable to overthrow God, his sole objective was now to destroy God's plans and God's creation. If Satan could not destroy God, he was going to destroy what God had created, and that would be us – you and me!

This brings us to the story of Adam and Eve in the Garden of Eden, and the forbidden fruit from the Tree of Knowledge of Good and Evil. The serpent, which was Satan, deceived Eve into believing that she too could be all knowledgeable just like God. And even though God had instructed Adam and Eve not to eat from that one tree, Satan twisted the words of God and made Eve question what God had really said and meant.

We all know the story. Eve and Adam ate the fruit from that tree, becoming the next victims of Satan's lies and deception, and opening a door for sin to enter into our world. Satan now had his way in to every human being that would ever walk the face of the earth.

Sin was now a part of our lives and our world and Satan would continue forever in his attempt to separate us from God in any way that he could.

This separation from God, which is caused by our sin, continues to grow each and every day when we choose to believe the lies and deceptions offered to us by Satan through the use of our free will. We eventually make choices that do not honor or glorify God. We then grow further and further away from God, the life that He had created us to live, and the person that He created us to be.

The War

The war that initially began in the Heavens thousands of years ago has been playing out in our lives each and every day. God created us to be perfect and pure, and to seek and follow Him. To be in complete union with Him and one with Him. However, at a very early point in our life, Satan jumps in and begins to plant the unsuspected seeds which will eventually begin to steer us away from God, and any desire to know or grow close to God. Yes, my friends, this is spiritual warfare.

I can see you cringing now. I know.... touchy subject. And that is exactly the problem. It is one that is rarely discussed anymore, and almost never taught or brought up in the modern-day church. This is the reason why we find it so difficult to accept nowadays when it does come up. Since it is rarely ever talked about, or taught, it must not really be a thing. It is just something that those 'crazy' people keep pushing. It is not the message that people want to hear.

People don't want the 'doom and gloom' gospel. We hate bad news. Unless of course it is happening to someone else, then we give it our full attention as it makes us feel better about the miserable life that we live. We just want the stuff that makes us feel good so that we can recharge and get back to living our normal everyday lives.

Just like you, I steered clear of any discussion on the subject for most all of my life. I did believe in God, and I even acknowledged that Satan was real. However, I knew very little about their relationship to each other or the impact that each one had on my life. I believed that if I just ignored Satan and did not acknowledge him, he would leave me alone.

This one belief just might be the most foolish and reckless choice that I had ever made, and believe me, I have made some doozies. Satan is real and Satan is going about his evil business every single day, whether we choose to acknowledge it or not. And if we simply choose not to believe that Satan has an impact on our lives, we are only fooling and deceiving ourselves.

Let me spell it out for those who may be struggling to connect the dots. This mentality is exactly what Satan wants. This is Satan's plan and by Satan's design. Simply ignoring or choosing not to acknowledge the fact that spiritual warfare is going on every day in our lives does not make it go away or mean that it does not exist. It is real, it is happening, and it is happening to every one of us every single day.

Satan is very much aware that if you and I acknowledge that spiritual warfare is a real thing which is playing out in our lives every day, we will then be aware of what is truly causing a vast majority of the issues in our life. And once we become aware of the source of the pain and suffering, we are obviously going to choose the alternative every time – which is exactly what Satan does not want us to do. Again, Satan does not want us seeking or choosing God, therefore he has to make sure that our perception, and what we see, is always distorted and inaccurate, making it appear that he is not involved at all and making us feel that our crappy life is just the cards we were dealt.

Satan is the master of deception. Deceiving us every single day to believe that what we do, what we choose, and what we perceive is always harmless and nothing that would lead us down a wrong path. If we were aware that we were being lied to and deceived, we would never fall for the deception to begin with. And it most always begins as simple little lies and deceptions which seem completely harmless and meaningless in and of themselves but eventually end up leading us further away from God.

And remember...... this happens to every one of us in this world and it has been happening to us since we were very young. We all become deceived at one point or another, we are all lied to and led astray. And our churches, places of worship, and religious activities which are so called 'holy' and 'righteous' are not exempt from these attacks either.

One result of this plague of lies and deceptions, is a world full of modern-day churches that not only fail to acknowledge spiritual warfare but know very little if anything about it. This too is Satan's plan and intention – to distort the Word and Image of God so that what we come to accept and believe as the truth is diametrically opposed to what reality actually is. Our modern-day churches and religious organizations have been misguided and deceived into believing a false perception of God and Jesus, and what reality truly is, just as we have.

The Wounds

As we mentioned previously, Satan begins these attacks on us at a very early point in our lives. Mostly so that he may inflict wounds upon us before we are able to obtain a solid foundation of God's Word and His Truths. These wounds cause us to alter our perspective, eventually changing the way in which we perceive others and what we perceive reality to be. The distortion of our perspective (that perspective which influences who we become) has already begun, and we will never see things the same way again.

Gradually, the seeds of the poser begin to take root. The minuscule and unnoticeable modifications to our inner beliefs are taking hold and reconstructing who we are and what we once believed. These seeds, which were planted in us by Satan, do not require much of his attention to fully blossom as we are excellent gardeners ourselves. They are like weeds that never seem to die, popping up in all of the places where we least desire them to be, and continuing to grow no matter how much we may try to kill them off.

That is, of course, if we are even aware of their existence, as most times we are not. Most always we just simply believe that these seeds - these new thoughts, actions, or behaviors – are just who we are and are just a part of our ever-changing life.

Without any outside influence in our lives that is supportive of the truths of reality, we begin to accept these new views and beliefs as our reality. And as that new reality or belief grows, we continually look for ways to validate or confirm that new belief, whether what we see as validation may be true or not.

Psychologists today refer to this as the confirmation bias. We look for ways to support or confirm a belief that we may have, whether that belief may be true or not.

This never-ending cycle continues to play out in our lives for decades. New seeds, new beliefs, a new perspective or view, and each one of them even more exponentially influenced by the multitude of previous seeds and false beliefs. Change is a constant at this point, always growing further and further away from the person that once was us.

Then, one day, somewhere in the middle of our lives, if we are fortunate, we wake up, completely lost and puzzled, and ask ourselves *"How in the world did I end up here?"*. I say 'fortunate' as for many people that day never comes. Some are never able to realize that they have strayed so far. Some are completely oblivious to what they have become and will even insist that this person that they are is who they truly were meant to be.

"Put on the full armor of God, so that you can take your stand against the devil's schemes. For our struggle is not against flesh and blood, but against the rulers, against the authorities, against the powers of this dark world and against the spiritual forces of evil in the heavenly realms. Therefore, put on the full armor of God, so that when the day of evil comes, you may be able to stand your ground, and after you have done everything, to stand." Ephesians 6:11-13

Chapter 4

The Main Ingredient

Now that we have somewhat of a basic understanding of what a poser is, let's see if we can grasp the why, or the reasoning for his/her existence.

Why does the poser exist? What is it that provokes us to make this change? And even more perplexing yet; how is one who is so utterly fake and counterfeit able to survive and flourish?

If we could remove the facade from our life, allowing ourselves to be fully exposed and truly honest, each of us would likely admit that we are nothing more than broken and damaged goods. I believe all of us have these feelings of self-worthlessness from time to time. All of us possess deep scars and wounds, which since the time of their arrival have shattered like a piece of broken glass into a thousand different fragments. Over time, little pieces of the initial wound are then broken off into even more fragments as we endure further attacks throughout our life. This is essentially who and what we are – thousands of little pieces of those traumatic events that we have endured, which have molded and shaped us, and which we have built our lives around.

We allow these wounds and fragments to define us. They control our thinking, shape our views, and determine which direction we move forward in life. They affect how we see other people and other things and also determine how we interact and respond to those other people and things. These fragments have a commanding effect on all of the choices and decisions that we make every single day.

The wounds and scars become our foundation, our cornerstone of the life that we then continue to build going forward. We make them our justification and rationale for everything that we do. Those little pieces of past wounds and scars essentially shape and form who we are and what we have become.

Many of us will find it hard to admit, and even difficult to see these wounds and scars. Many others will insist that they have not allowed their past to define who they are today and will even go on to insist that their life is going just as they planned. Well, Congratulations! You too, my friend, have mastered the life of the poser! You have become so good at the charade that you even have yourself fooled.

The Roots

The life of the poser commences much like that of anyone else. There are but a few fundamental needs which all of us innately possess. Needs which we cannot live without, and that are essential to our existence. Needs that we will spend our entire lives in search of no matter who we are or what we do.

There are five basic necessities of life which are required for our survival. Food, water, shelter, clothing, and air. While clothing could be debatable given the right environment, these essential elements ensure our physiological survival. However, the fundamental needs we are referring to ensure our sociological survival, which ensures our physical and psychological well-being, rather than a mere biological existence.

In 1943, psychology professor Abraham Maslow formulated *'Maslow's Hierarchy of Needs'*[1] based on his original paper *'A Theory of Human Motivation'*[2].

Maslow's hierarchy is a conceptualization of the needs that motivate human behavior. These needs are what each of us innately possess, what we shape our entire existence around, and what drives all of us to become the poser.

All of us crave, need, and desire the love, attention, and admiration of others. And we simply cannot live without it. Those who have tried are left with an empty, soulless life that is void of any joy or sustenance at all. We all need people in our lives, and deep down, our hearts know this to be true.

I know this can be a challenge for many of us to embrace, as I am not a big fan of other people myself at times. However, this innate value is a part of our creation – it is who we are to our core and essential to our existence. And while the intention of this value was for a much greater purpose, we do not have the ability to ignore it or make it go away, no matter how hard we may try.

So, despite the fact that our mind may be telling us that we do not need these other people, and that we do not want to get close to others, our soul keeps pushing us forward in search of this love, attention, and admiration. We are constantly seeking it out in everything that we do, whether doing so consciously or subconsciously. Whether it be in the activities, tasks, work that we do, or in the people that we befriend, follow, associate with or encounter – one inherent quality is the constant motivating factor moving us to think, act, and respond in the way that we do, and to make the choices and decisions that we do.

This need, this desire, this craving is something that each of us is born with. It is part of who we are. It is in our DNA. And by simple deduction, we do not have the ability to create a person or the inner workings of a human being, therefore, we do not have the ability to change or alter the way in which one has been created either. So, no matter how hard we may try, we cannot make it go away. We may push it down, we may try to suppress it, and we may even deny its existence all together – but it is still there, deep inside each and every one of us, always having some influence on who we are.

In his book, *The Divine Conspiracy*, the late Dallas Willard states: "Truth must yield to desire, which drives the psychic (human) community."[3]

> "Human love has little regard for truth. It makes the truth relative, since nothing, not even the truth, must come between it and the be-loved..."[4]

As human beings, we instinctively modify what the truth is to suit our own pleasures and desires. We will knowingly alter truth or reality, making it whatever we need it to be, so that we are able to fulfill our own pleasures and desires.

This one inherent quality that each and every one of us possess is desire. Desire is the main ingredient and the seed for the creation of the poser. We must understand, though, that this quality is not in and of itself a bad thing. It is surely a good thing, for all things made by our Creator are good. It is us, mankind, and our sinful nature which takes these good things and utilizes them for a purpose other than what they were created for.

The Development

Because we're born with this desire, it shapes our lives from a very early age. It is also no coincidence that Satan, sin, and the attacks upon us, with their correlating wounds, begin to occur at this early stage in life. We'll explore those attacks and the resulting wounds in more detail in later chapters. For now, just remember that our need and desire for love, attention, and admiration can easily be distorted by these attacks.

The seed, or the main ingredient for the creation of the poser, once again, exists in every one of us. That seed is our desire to be loved, to be wanted, to be admired, and to be acknowledged or accepted. We want...... No, we desire for others to like us, to accept us, to admire us, and to provide us validation. We crave it like nothing else. And this is exactly what we'll end up spending our entire lives searching for.

Take a moment to reflect on that idea. From the time a child is born, that child wants only to be held and touched by its mother. For the next couple years that child will cry and scream, only to get someone's attention, so that someone may pick them up, hold them, and show them love and attention. As the child becomes a toddler, a stage in life when they are learning new things every day, that child will now immediately turn their head to an elder when doing something new, seeking validation and affirmation that they have done right.

This desire does not stop as we grow into our teenage years and beyond. The only thing that does change at this point is who and what we perceive we need to get this validation from, and who's attention it is that we are trying to obtain. The cycle continues, day after day, for the rest of our lives. What and who we chase after to garner this love, admiration and validation is constantly changing as we quickly abandon one thing or person for another when we are once again left feeling empty and abandoned. Always seeking, always searching, always looking to fill that empty chasm in our soul which desires only to be truly loved.

Eventually, we find ourselves in the last days of our life, with no one around, desiring more than anything to have just one true, authentic person to spend our last moments with.

Degrees of Separation

As I've mentioned, and you are hopefully beginning to realize, we're all posers. It is the way of this world, and the way that we have been indoctrinated into living our life in this world. While every one of us is a poser, there is no one set model for the poser and not all of us have become the 'full-blown' poser. The different levels and degrees of the poser life can be just as diverse as the different cultures that we see in our world today. And just like those different cultures, it is the environment that each poser was brought up in which determines the extent and traits that each poser will acquire and possess.

Much of the poser's existence is shaped by their personal view of the world that they live in, or their surroundings. How they see things, how they experience things, and how they come to understand and perceive these different experiences. And since all of us see, experience, and understand all things differently; each of us, therefore, will have these impressions influence us in a different manner as well. It is what we see, or what we believe that we see, which determines the extent or severity of each individual poser.

The truth of the matter is that most all of us are unable to see what reality actually is. I'm aware that many of you may find that statement hard to accept; believing that reality is what plays out right in front of us and is what we experience every single day. Therein lies our problem. The things that we see and the things that we experience every single day are almost always not true reality; or a true representation of what is actually going on. These are simply the things we're being led to believe and accept as reality. They are a lie. They are a falsehood. They are a ruse, a deception. I understand that this may be a bit hard to grasp at this point but hang in there and we will get a better grasp of this truth as we go along.

The degree or extent of change in the individual poser is highly influenced by how skewed his or her understanding and acceptance of this false reality is. The more convinced the individual is of this false reality, the greater the depth of their life as a poser.

The Flaw

For each individual poser, it becomes a matter of their perception. How they see and perceive the events and occurrences in their life, and what they interpret those happenings to mean. Each interpretation will then directly cause a change within that individual that is proportionate to the degree that the event or happening was distorted. We then begin to have a misconstrued view and outlook on all future matters as the information from this one event that we have now stored in our minds, which we use as a guide in making decisions and choices, is now flawed and inaccurate. As we move forward in life, every single little thing that we see, experience, and encounter will now be viewed with this faulty perspective.

The matter compounds itself exponentially as we move forward in life, continuing to make new conclusions through the use of those faulty beliefs which we have allowed ourselves to adopt as our reality. We are now forming new opinions and beliefs based upon our previous erroneous beliefs. Therefore, the new beliefs which we now obtain that were gathered with a tainted and inadequate perspective are more so flawed than the previous beliefs. The cycle never ends; it only becomes progressively more warped as time goes on.

Then, seemingly out of nowhere, we wake up one day and find it perfectly normal and acceptable that a so-called grown man can use the same public restroom as an eight-year-old girl, at the same time. We accept and even give in to the ideology that having only two genders is offensive.

It is all the same, whether it be on a personal level, or a worldly level. The flaw which we have is in our perception. Our perception of what reality truly is has been distorted since we were very young. And the level of distortion only increases as we move on through life.

Again, it is not so much the actual events or occurrences which directly impact our future. It is in the way that we perceive those events or occurrences which greatly shapes and influences our lives moving forward.

Let's go back to the last chapter and revisit that key phrase once again: ***"The way in which we perceive that action or occurrence and how we then allow it to affect our view of reality."***

Take a pause for a moment and ask yourself:
 "What false reality have I allowed myself to believe?"
 "What lies and deceptions have I fallen victim too?"

The Outcome

The severity of these attacks and the depth of our new poser persona are directly related to the extent of our belief in the lies and/or deceptions which we have come to assume as our new reality.

As was mentioned in the previous chapter, there are countless variations of the poser, each having a different level or degree of modification. From the *periodic poser* who only on occasion brings out their new persona, to the *full-blown poser* who has completely changed everything in and around their life, with scores of other mutations in-between.

What we must understand, however, is that these different classifications are merely a label, signifying the extent or depth of the change or alteration. These labels basically give an indication of how deeply the person has bought into the lies and deceptions which they have been confronted with. What these classifications do not foretell is how that person has perceived those lies and deceptions to harm them, and therefore, to what extreme their new poser persona will be.

Take my life as an example. I was considered to be a *full-blown poser*. I lived my life for myself, just trying to survive, and doing whatever I had to so that I would fit in and hopefully gain an advantage. I lied to people, cheated people, conned people, stole from people, and inflicted quite a bit of harm to many others. I did and became what I felt was necessary to survive and get a leg up on other people. What I am able to realize now is that I did these things and acted in this manner as a reaction to the wounds that I had received when I was young – and the way in which I perceived those wounds to affect my reality.

I bought into the lies that I wasn't good enough, and that no one loved me. I bought into the deception that no one wanted to be around me, and that I was on my own. I bought into the accusations that I was worthless and would never amount to anything. These became my new beliefs, whether they were true or not. And since these were my new perceptions, the way in which I would view everything going forward would be through a lens of these new convictions.

However, there are a multitude of *full-blown posers* out there, and due to their wounds and the ways in which they perceived them, their life as a poser may have taken a much different course. The *full-blown poser* subtype would also include those who are murderers, rapists, pedophiles, drug dealers, and the likes.

Again, the classification is merely a label. It is how each individual perceives their wounds which will determine the extent and depth of their change.

A Personal Note

A few days ago, my wife and I received a phone call from someone who is very close to us. He asked if there was a time that would be convenient for us to have a video call with him and his wife, as they had something that they wanted to share with us. We both agreed to being available later that evening.

Several hours later, the time had come, and my wife and I placed the call using one of the video chat apps on her phone. My friend and his wife answered the call and were well prepared having put all distractions aside. After a short period of catching up and small chit-chat, my friend stated that they had something that they wanted to share with us. My wife and I both knew that it had to be something significant, as openly sharing the happenings in their life was not the norm for these two.

My friend then informed us that after ten years of being married, they had decided that a separation would be best for both of them, as well as their two little girls. They went on to say that they had talked things through respectfully, and that they were going to remain friends while trying to keep the process as amicable as possible. They also talked about the kids and the steps they had taken to avoid disrupting their lives. They had every little detail planned out in an effort to make a separation feel and appear as though nothing happened at all.

We have known this 'friend' for all of his life. We had also known his wife for several years prior to them getting married. We knew who they were, what they stood for, and could fairly precisely predict which direction they would go on just about any matter. But this was unexpected. While my wife and I had noticed some issues of concern over the past few years in their relationship, this was far from what either of us had anticipated or wanted.

Through the video call, I could see the pain in the eyes of my friend. It was well suppressed, and I don't believe that he was fully aware of what was inside him trying so badly to get out. I quickly got the feeling that there had to be something more going on here, and most likely, this young couple wasn't even aware of it. I had to dive in deeper. I had to see if there was anything we could do to help. After all, we love this couple like family and the last thing we would ever want to see in their lives is separation.

So I spoke up and asked if they could tell me why, and what it was that brought this about. They both turned to look at each other with reluctance and then turned back to face the camera. My friend's wife then provided a response which caused me to pull my head back in shock and disbelief. She stated that she has realized that she is gay, and out of respect for each other and their individual desires, they feel it would be best to separate.

My wife and I realized that there was not much we could do in the moment, other than offer our support and love. We tried to encourage them while giving some advice on how best to move forward at this point, not only for them, but for their two little girls as well. Then we ended the call and began to pray.

Maybe a little bit of backstory would help, as it provides foundational reasoning for the events which played out. My friends' wife is employed by her mother, who owns and runs multiple upscale salons. It has become more and more common in modern times that the stylists and other employees working at these salons are not heterosexual. Therefore, over the past few years, my friends' wife has been immersed into this lifestyle, while having the beliefs and views of this lifestyle become her entire day. (Remember the quote from Chapter 1 – *"We are all a product of our own environment"*) I must also inject that at no point in her life prior to working for her mother did she ever have, show, acknowledge, or express any interest in this lifestyle or others of the same sex.

My wife and I continued to pray for this couple and their family, and we will not stop praying for them. I am sure that Psychologists and Counselors alike could raise many questions to the couple in an effort to find other reasons for their breakup. However, this was a good family unit. Both my friend and his wife had good, stable jobs with good income and no financial struggles. They lived within their means and enjoyed vacations and family time together. They both love their little girls more than anything. And they both loved and were committed to each other from the start.

The not so simple answer to the *Why* is Satan. It is Satan, along with his evil spirits, demons, and the forces of darkness. All using lies and deceptions to pull us away from God and the life that God has planned for us. God created union between a man and a woman, and He cherishes it greatly. Therefore, because God created it, Satan wants to destroy it.

My friends' wife went from being a strong, loving, committed spouse and mother – to believing a lie and a story that she was actually something else. And she believed that lie so much that she was willing to throw away her family and everything they had built together in exchange for it.

What is it that we allow ourselves to see and believe from these events that causes us so much trauma? The answer to this question is not so much *'What'* we see, but *'Why'* we see it the way that we do.

We perceive these events and occurrences the way we do as a result of the wounds which were inflicted upon us at a young age by Satan.

These wounds cause us to build a protective shield around our lives in an effort to never experience that hurt again.

These wounds radically distort our perspective, and the ways in which we perceive things to be.

These wounds, at an early age, derail our lives from the intended path that it was set on. And much like a powerful locomotive, once we have been derailed, we cannot get back on to those tracks by ourselves.

"For everything that is in the world does not come from the Father. The desires of our flesh and the things our eyes see and want and the pride of this life come from the world." 1 John 2:16 NLV

Chapter 5

The Wounds

We have already established that Satan is our enemy, simply by deriving that we are all a creation of God, and that Satan is at war with God. Since Satan can no longer directly attack God, he continues this war by attacking and attempting to destroy anything that God has created. Satan is also committed to impeding anyone from knowing the truth about God and/or growing close to God, and he does so through the manipulation of our free will.

As we take a closer look into the wounds which begin to drastically alter and distort our perspective from a very early point in our lives, we must first possess a basic understanding of this war that we find ourselves stuck in, and how that war shapes and influences our future outcome, and the life of the poser.

Some of you, however, may be distracted with questions that are beginning to surface in your mind, such as:

- *I already believe in God. Am I not protected by God from these attacks?*

- *What is the point of believing in God if I am going to be attacked anyways?*

- *If God actually does have control over all things, why does He allow Satan to attack us?*

These are all legitimate questions. Questions which I had as well prior to God revealing His truths to me. The war, and spiritual warfare, can be a very complex subject. This one chapter, or even this entire book, would be far from sufficient in providing a complete understanding of the matter. For the sake of simplicity, we will just scratch the surface for now, discussing a few key points and fundamentals. However, I would strongly suggest that you seek a deeper awareness so that you too may be better equipped in the battles that we face every day.

Two books which I highly recommend are:
— *The Bondage Breaker* by Dr. Neil Anderson[1]
— *The Handbook For Spiritual Warfare* by Dr. Ed Murphy[2]

Answers

To answer our questions from above, we need to have at least a basic understanding of what a war is, as well as how that war, or any war for that matter, actually plays out. A war is the confrontation of two or more opposing forces, with each force seeking to dominate and overtake the opposing force for the purpose of achieving their goal.

The Merriam-Webster dictionary defines *war* as:
a: a state of hostility, conflict, or antagonism
b: a struggle or competition between opposing forces or for a particular end[3]

A war is the broad, all-encompassing action which consists of countless individual battles or skirmishes that take place in an effort for one side to gain control or dominance. With every war, and nearly every battle, casualties are inevitable and almost a certainty. Most all of us today have some knowledge or awareness of World War II, the deadliest war in history. No matter which side you may have been on, no matter which country you may have fought for; casualties occurred on a daily basis. Casualties ranging anywhere from a simple cut or bodily wound to the ultimate loss, that of one's life.

During World War II, with the rare exception, every casualty that did occur happened while that individual was fighting for or seeking to advance the cause of his/her side, and while that individual was following the orders and direction of their commanders. And every commander, regardless of which side they may be on, fully supported their troops which they had sent into each battle. Every commander would also take the appropriate actions which they perceived to be best in helping their side to be successful in these battles.

So, to answer our first question – *I already believe in God. Am I not protected by God from these attacks?*

The simple answer to that question is.... Yes. You are protected by God. However, protection does not imply immunity. It is a war, and we will be attacked, simply because we are on the opposing side. And yes, casualties will occur even while we are under the protection of God, our loving Father. Just as the commanders and leaders in World War II fully supported their troops and did not wish to lose one of them, casualties happened, and lives were lost.

One thing which we must learn to recognize though, is why these attacks happen. We cannot be successful in any battle that we face if; we do not know our opponents' skills and abilities and know what our opponents' goal or intention is. We must learn to see the real reason why we are being attacked, and who is actually attacking us.

For most of us, we take these attacks personally, as if the offender is out to harm us directly. We immediately become defensive and either retaliate or allow that attack to change our attitude and emotions. We do not know who our enemy is so we fight back against the person who has caused us the pain or suffering – most always the one standing right in front of us.

We are also unable to see the true reasoning behind these attacks. Due to our skewed perspective of this world and of ourselves, which we will come to have a better understanding of later in this chapter, we create illogical reasons as to why we are undergoing these attacks.

The truth is that all attacks come from Satan, in one form or another, with the sole intention of separating us from God. Satan does not have one ounce of care for you, for who you are, or for what you call your life. Satan's only care is to do anything and everything that he can to get you to turn from God, to question God, or to think that there is a better life without God.

The Apostle Paul makes it very clear who our enemy is in Ephesians 6:12: *"For our struggle is not against flesh and blood, but against the rulers, against the authorities, against the powers of this dark world and against the spiritual forces of evil in the heavenly realms."*

Satan can attack us, even as believers in Christ who are already saved. And yes, God does protect us and even equips us with the tools and weapons to fight back in these battles. However, it is only through Jesus Christ that we will ever be successful in these battles. If we are not in Christ, and God, we have already lost the battle to an opponent who is more powerful than we will ever be on our own.

Which then leads us to our second question – *What is the point of believing in God if I am going to be attacked anyways?*

There are countless reasons to believe in God and accept Jesus Christ as your Lord and Savior. The primary reason being that God is who we were created by and created for. Each and every one of us was created by God, in the image of God, with the sole purpose of honoring and glorifying God. Our fight in the war between God and Satan, and the attacks that confront us every day, are simply a result of who we are and the family that we are a part of – the family of God.

And finally, the question that most non-believers and many new believers struggle with – *If God actually does have control over all things, why does He allow Satan to attack us?*

Once again, a major stumbling block which each of us possess lies within our perspective. The ways in which we see, understand, and relate to all things is broken, or faulty to say the least. It is as if we are wearing a pair of reading glasses that are shattered or cracked. We are only able to see fragments, or bits and pieces of this life. We then take those fragments and attempt to assemble them in our minds into something that makes sense to us, something that we are able to understand or relate to – most always resulting in a perspective or understanding that is nowhere near reality.

So, when we ask why God allows something to happen, and then allow ourselves to come up with a reasoning for that occurrence, our reasoning is almost always nowhere near what the reality of the matter is. We do not see the big picture; we are only seeing bits and pieces. God is God, the Creator and Ruler of all things. His knowledge of all things is infinite as well.

God tells us in Isaiah 55:8-9:
[8] *"For my thoughts are not your thoughts, neither are your ways my ways," declares the Lord.* [9] *"As the heavens are higher than the earth, so are my ways higher than your ways and my thoughts than your thoughts."*

These are valid yet tough questions and a short paragraph or two does not adequately provide an sufficient response. However, I am hoping that they may leave you with a desire to know more. There are many great authors out there today with a wealth of knowledge and accurate information. One of my personal favorites is John Eldredge. John has written thirty-eight books to date, and founded *WildatHeart.org* based off his best-selling book *Wild at Heart*.[4] John's books are what I would call an 'easy read'. While they are all chock-full of life-giving information, they are not difficult to get through.

Another of my favorites is the late Dallas Willard. And while some parts of his countless books may be a challenge, Dallas shares a perspective and understanding that only a few are able to obtain.

Being a Child

As we are brought into this world at birth, it is as if we have been dropped behind enemy lines during the height of World War II. We don't know where we are, and we surely haven't been given a battle plan. Heck – we're not even aware that there is a war going on. From this early age in our lives we begin adapting to the environment around us, just simply trying to survive.

The enemy has been fighting this battle for thousands of years prior to our arrival and knows every square inch of the battlefield. He does not want us to become the strong warrior that we were created to be, so from a very early age in our lives the attacks begin.

Now remember – this is all new to us. We have no experience at anything and are simply trying to learn as we go through the events and occurrences happening around us. Our young, naive, impressionable minds. Unable to differentiate between right and wrong, good and bad, truth or lies – for we have not yet been taught or obtained a basis for any of the above. At this point in our lives it is rather easy to deceive us with simple little lies and falsehoods. Lies which we come to accept as being the truth as we keep hearing and seeing them over and over again. These lies and falsehoods soon become our reality and what we come to believe as being true reality.

It does not take much to alter our course at this stage in our life. A little thought planted here and there. A little pain inflicted by someone that we love. Or simply the unmet need of our own personal expectations. We then take those thoughts, that pain, that rejection – and we run with it in our own minds allowing it to grow into something that we can no longer control.

These wounds and this pain have now become a part of our constitution. It is who we are, and we allow it to define who we become as we grow older. The transformation to our life as a poser has just begun, at such a young age, and unbeknownst to us.

Think back to the time when you were just a child. For some of us, this is no longer possible as we have buried those memories so deeply that we are completely unaware that they still exist. Or better yet just observe a young child as they go about their day.

A child that has not yet been fully poisoned by the ways of the world is a complete joy to encounter. I would think that many of us occasionally find ourselves watching a child play, recalling that long lost feeling of joy and innocence, only to find ourselves wishing that we could capture those same feelings just one more time.

That child is carefree, outgoing, and fully open to those around them. That child does not place judgment on the others around them, or label them with a race, color, social or financial status. That child does not care if the other comes from the ghetto or the prosperous side of town. That child does not care if the other is wearing the latest designer fashions or hand-me-downs from their older sibling. That child simply sees another person, and another chance to enjoy life to its fullest, all while having no predetermined expectations, plans, or motives.

That, my friends, is who we were truly created to be. Completely carefree, open, loving, and non-judgmental. Openly taking life and every situation as it comes to us, without a predetermined plan or ulterior motive for our personal benefit or gain. That is the life we were given, and the life that we could and should be living even as grown adults.

I am sure that last sentence may have many of you questioning my perspective right about now. This is normal. Well, normal for the world that we live in. We learn from a very young age that we are to get an education, get a job, and then grow up and do responsible, respectful adult things. We are taught not to act like a child as we get older as it makes us look foolish, immature, and unwise. How many times have you heard or been told – *'Grow up', 'Be a man', 'Stop acting like a child'*?

We are indirectly given a set of rules and guidelines on how our life should play out and what that life should look like long before we ever make it through puberty. We unknowingly integrate the behaviors and tendencies of others into our way of thinking, once again, as we are a product of the environment that we exist in. Therefore, we too come to accept these teachings and expectations as our reality. The way things must truly be. A reality governed and controlled by the expectations of how others and the world wish for us to live.

So, dismissing the characteristics of a child's life as we grow older is something that we have been taught or programmed to accept as being normal, and something that we must do. We are only doing what everyone else has taught us to do, and what everyone else is doing as well. Once again, we are just trying to fit in and gain acceptance.

In the 18th chapter of the book of Matthew, Jesus provides us with some invaluable advice on how we should live our lives. The disciples had come to Jesus with a question – [1]*"Who, then, is the greatest in the kingdom of Heaven?"* Jesus then called a little child over and said to the disciples: [3]*"Truly I tell you, unless you change and become like little children, you will never enter the kingdom of heaven."*

I am not implying that we should remove all responsibility and obligation from our lives as an adult, and neither was Jesus. This, in fact, is one of the major problems with the next generation coming up – they have not been taught how to take or accept responsibility for their actions or behaviors. We fully need these responsibilities and obligations for many reasons. Most importantly, we need them as they teach us to respect and love the others around us.

Jesus was stating that we needed to return to having the child-like qualities that we once had. Qualities such as trust, believing without seeing, and having faith without the predetermined expectations or assurances that we insist on as an adult. Jesus was also stating that we have become 'know-it-all's' and that we should relearn how to be naive once again. Children know that they do not have all the answers, and they are okay with that.

Our constant search for knowledge and our need to always have an answer to every question has turned us into people that do not feel the need for God as we already know everything there is to know......... and if we don't, we can find the answer within three clicks of a mouse.

The Scars

As most all of us have come to learn through our adult lives, we run a much greater risk of being hurt when we allow ourselves to be completely open to others. However, this complete vulnerability is the only way that we are able to experience a deep and meaningful relationship with another person. We fully expose ourselves to others, allowing them access to the most private and reserved parts of our heart and soul. These are the areas within us where an everlasting bond and relationship exist.

Unfortunately, as we do reveal ourselves to others, allowing them into these special places, we also expose ourselves to the potential of a deep and painful wound. Damage inflicted at this level of our soul does not heal quickly, or easily. Any wound that we receive will most certainly leave a long-lasting scar which has the sole purpose to remind us daily of the pain and suffering which we endured the last time we allowed someone into this special place. We then close the door to that part of our heart and soul, lock it, and swear to never let anyone else in again.

Yes, we may eliminate the potential for deep wounds and scars. But in our attempt of self-preservation, we also eliminate the possibility of any deep, meaningful relationship, which is the only place where true love and joy are found. The pain and suffering that we experienced from our initial wounds were so severe that we are now willing to sacrifice joy and happiness for the rest of our lives just so that we don't have to endure that pain again. The pain from the initial wound was more than we could bear.......... or was it? Well, that is how we perceived it to be. However, as we are beginning to learn, our perception is faulty and flawed as well.

As we discussed a few pages back, Satan begins these attacks on our lives during our childhood. These attacks come in a myriad of ways, each being dependent upon what the individual person sees and values as being important or cherished. Satan aims to wound us where it will hurt us the most. Satan is out to mortally wound each and every one of us. In other words - Satan goes in for the kill on every attack - to take us out of the fight, eliminating the potential for us to realize our true purpose in life, and to take us away from the life that God had planned for us.

Satan's attacks are not designed to simply give us a minor wound, one which we could easily shrug off in a short period of time. His attacks are intended to leave us scarred for the rest of our lives, altering our direction and trajectory and completely changing the outcome of who and what we are.

With the severity of the wounds that are inflicted upon us, one would assume that the attacks should be obvious and evident. We must not forget – Satan is the master of lies and deception. It is in this deception that we are unable to recognize these attacks for what they truly are, and where the attacks are truly coming from, causing us to enter into a conflict with someone or something other than our true opponent. If we were able to recognize the deception that was occurring and where the attack was truly coming from, even the most foolish and simple-minded of us would be reluctant to fall for the deceptions to begin with.

I know the thought that many of you are having right now as it is the same one that I believed for many years. *I'm smarter than that! I'm smart enough to realize when someone is lying to me, and smart enough to see that I am being deceived.*

Yet again, we underestimate the power of our enemy. Our enemy who at one point was the second most powerful angel in all of creation. Our enemy who knows this world and the spiritual world better than anyone other than God himself. Our enemy who has studied your every move since the day you were born. C'mon people. Really!! Stop being so naive. We unsuspectingly fall victim to the cons and deceptions used in the simple advertising of products on television and social media every single day. We really don't have a clue when and if we are being deceived. And we really don't stand a chance on our own! We are never going to outsmart Satan and the forces of darkness on our own – and we were never meant to.

Therefore, Satan will most always begin these attacks with a little 'jab' here and a little 'jab' there. Just enough to cause some pain in our lives and redirect our thoughts. And once Satan has that initial thought, question, or doubt planted into our minds it is pretty much game over. It now becomes rather easy for Satan to build upon and compound those thoughts, most times without having to do anything further as we will begin to do all of the work for him.

We allow our confirmation bias to take over and suddenly begin to look for ways to validate that initial lie or deception in the experiences which we have moving forward. Instead of recognizing that lie or deception for what it truly is, we accept that lie or deception as being the truth and seek out ways to validate its authenticity and make it our reality – whether those ways may be credible or not. Sooner than later, we turn that lie or deception into our new reality – a false reality that we then build our lives around.

Simply put, we come to accept all of the struggles and difficulties in our life, which are often an attack from the kingdom of darkness, and we normalize them, adapting our lives to them, eventually creating a new us – The Poser.

As we have learned, these attacks and the wounds which they inflict come in a multitude of ways. It would not be possible to list out every single method and type of attack that Satan brings against us. However, they all have one underlying purpose – to alter or change the person who we are in such a way that it causes us to become something other than who we were created to be. It is through this purpose that the life of the poser is created – sending us down a path that takes us far away from the person that we were created to be.

We have also discovered that for the majority of us, these attacks begin at a very young age. We are uneducated, uninformed, and lacking in knowledge and experience. We are naive, innocent, and very open and trusting. We absorb every bit of information presented to us in an attempt to learn about this new world that we are now a part of. This innocence, this naivety, this openness leaves us vulnerable and an easy target for Satan to plant a little seed or inflict just a little wound which will metastasize until it consumes our entire being.

For some of us it may have been seeing your alcoholic father beat your mother over and over again. Others may have had to endure the perverted relative who took pleasure in touching little children. It could have been an overbearing schoolteacher, a pastor at your church who took his calling and used it as a power grab over his congregation, or maybe a neighbor down the street who was a bit too friendly and welcoming or demeaning and abusing. It could have been that little girl/boy who you so badly had a crush on but rejected you time and time again. These are but a few of those moments from our past when the wounds were inflicted, and unbeknownst to us at the time, the course of our lives would forever be changed. These are but a few of those moments where each one of us lost our innocence – that point in time when we abruptly realized that this world was not such a good place. That point in time when we stopped being open and trusting, and out of self-preservation, became guarded and defensive.

For most of us however, it is not just one single event or moment which brings about our change. It is multiple events, experiences, or moments over time which continue to erode away our soul. The initial event or experience is just the trigger which opens the door for us to see or perceive the events and experiences which will follow in the ways that we then do. The initial wound is for nothing other than to distort our view of reality so that we may perceive the ensuing events as Satan wishes us to see them – that as being our new reality, our new false reality.

For me, that first wound was given through my parents. Having a father that would soon leave my mother and their four children so that he could chase after another woman, and her kids. Just as he had done previously when he chased after my mother. This would leave my mother to raise four children on her own, which meant working multiple jobs, and never being at home. I was deprived of the love and attention that a young child so badly needs from their parents. I had also been denied the teachings, direction, and validation from a father that a boy so desperately needs to mature into a confident young man.

Such an easy target for Satan and his attacks. The seeds were then planted, which I continually validated with my newly modified perspective in the coming encounters of my life. I quickly made it my reality that nobody wanted me, nobody wanted to be around me, nobody liked me, and that I was not good enough for anyone or in anything that I did. This was now who I was and what

I had accepted to be my reality. I had allowed myself to fall victim to the lies and deceptions and then began the change of who I was to accommodate this newly perceived reality.

I would then spend the better part of the next fifty years trying to obtain love, respect, admiration and validation from others. And since every person and every situation was different, I would continually modify who I was in an effort to become someone that I believed would be more attractive or desirable to that specific person or situation; only to ease the pain of the wound which had inflicted me.

That is what I believed reality to be, and I allowed that new reality to redirect and define my entire life. In actuality, the true reality was that my father had issues of his own and only noticed his own self pleasure and desires. The true reality was that my mother was forced into a position of being the sole provider for her four children which kept her away from home and her children most of the time, which I am sure was not an easy choice to make.

The true reality was not that no one desired me, it was that I just happened to have parents who did not have the best guidance or direction themselves, and who had also been greatly deceived by Satan as well. The true reality was that this one situation had no effect on how others would view me, even though I perceived it to be that way. The true reality is that there were several good men in my life over the years, and while they may not have been my father, each of them left their fingerprints on my life, impacting who I would come to be.

Once again – we all experience these wounds in our lives. It is not the actual wounds which hold us back and hinder our growth and potential as it is the way in which we perceive these wounds and then allow that new perception to alter who we are.

We need to accept and acknowledge where these wounds truly originate from, accept the fact that they are a part of our life, and then firmly believe that these wounds do not determine or define who we are as a person.

Once we allow ourselves to completely embrace the fact that Satan is actively involved in our lives and our world, it can be a bit overwhelming. We are essentially giving in to an idea that a being far more powerful than we are has the ability to wreak havoc on our lives whenever he so choses. Well, that is reality my friends, and there is nothing we can do to change it. There are many things in this world and our existence which are far greater than we are. We didn't make the rules. We didn't create the world. And we do not get to decide how everything plays out.

There is a positive side to embracing this reality, however. And it comes in two ways.

First – simply knowing and believing that Satan is actively involved in our lives should give us some relief. Wait! Is that correct? Relief? Yes, relief. Understanding that Satan is working against us and our lives every day means that the majority of the struggles and difficulties that we face are not solely because we have a crappy life or are a bad person. They are coming from an external source. They are not who WE are. The relief is seeing that we may not be as messed up as we actually think we are.

Second – when we accept Jesus Christ as our Lord and Savior, Satan and the powers of darkness no longer have a hold on us. They no longer have the ability to control our lives. Sure, we will still be attacked, and probably even more so than before as we are now seeing what Satan doesn't want us to see. However, in Christ, we now have the powers and the abilities to fight back, and to win that fight.

"We know that we are children of God, and that the whole world is under the control of the evil one." 1 John 5:19

Chapter 6

Do You See What I See?

"Few people have the imagination for reality"
Johann Wolfgang von Geothe (1749-1832)

As we learned in the previous chapter, no one is safe from these attacks, so the resulting wounds are a certainty for all of us. Each and every one of us have wounds, and many of us bear multiple wounds received from numerous attacks over the years. In all likelihood, most of us have also become completely oblivious to the majority of the wounds which we retain, as well as how those wounds have affected us and how they have shaped and transformed our lives.

So, how is it possible that something which we may only be subconsciously aware of can lead us to alter or change the characteristics and qualities of who we are? And more importantly, why do we allow this change to occur if the reasoning for the change is something which we are not giving any conscious thought too?

The Human Mind

Our brain is the most powerful organ ever created. Having over 100 billion neurons (nerve cells) which communicate through trillions of connections. The information in our brain can travel at speeds up to 350 miles per hour. It is also a myth that we only utilize roughly 10% of our brain. We actually use all of it, even when we are sleeping.[1]

In regard to our thought processes, we have two sides to our brain. That of conscious thought and that of subconscious thought.

Our conscious thoughts are the ones that we are aware of and thinking about at any given moment. Also known as a state of awareness where we are actively processing information with the ability to reflect on our own mental activity. This includes activities like planning, making decisions, and engaging in self-reflection.

Our subconscious mind operates beneath our level of conscious awareness, influencing our thoughts, feelings, and actions without us actively having to think about them. A few examples include our habits, emotional reactions, and even how we react in certain situations. It's like a hidden 'program' that runs in the background, continually processing information and guiding our behavior.

Sudden feelings of fear, joy, or anger, which are often triggered by past experiences stored in our subconscious, can be examples of subconscious emotional responses. These reactions can be instantaneous and not fully explained by our conscious thought.

The subconscious mind stores a vast array of memories, beliefs, and fears, some of which may be difficult to access directly through our conscious thought. However, these subconscious thoughts can still influence our behavior and perceptions. The subconscious mind is constantly working, even when we are asleep, processing information and influencing our thoughts and actions. Psychologists believe that 90% of our thoughts and behaviors come from our subconscious mind.

Those wounds, and the scars that they left behind, which all of us received at some early point in our lives are stored in our subconscious – the part of our brain which operates on its own without any effort from us. Constantly running and always calculating an easier, more efficient, safer and more predictable direction for our lives. That is the job of our subconscious mind – to survive, or to help us survive and keep us alive.

The human mind is also very reactive. The brain is constantly processing information from our environment and responding to that information. This includes both conscious and subconscious reactions to stimuli, such as physical sensations, emotions, and external events. Our brain is also highly adaptive and constantly evolving to better interact with the environment that we are a part of.

Hmmmm....... might we be on to something here. The brain is constantly evolving, or changing, to adapt to its environment. But the part of the brain which does most all of the changing is the subconscious, which appears to run on its own? So how can we ever stop changing or becoming something other than what we are today if we don't have control over the part of our brain that is initiating the change to begin with?

The good news is that we can stop the change; or at least redirect the subconscious modifications in a way that allows them to become beneficial to our growth instead of detrimental to who we are. Not all change is bad. All of us need change, or improvement in who we are as a person. And as long as that change which we are initiating is with the intent to better the person who we are, without transforming us into someone completely different, that change is a good thing.

All we need to do is learn how to become a computer programmer. Well, in a theoretical sense. This is actually much easier than it may sound. Many of us in this day and age do not possess the working knowledge of a computer however, especially those of the older generation. Ya, we know how to turn one on, and we may even find our way through the programs or apps that we utilize on a daily basis. But once that computer begins to operate in a way that we are not accustomed too, we simply don't have a clue what to do.

The computer, much like our lives and our mind, has that 'program' running in the background which controls or directs the overall operation, functions, and purpose of that computer. This 'program' is known as an operating system. And just like you and I, there are a multitude of computers operating in our world every day, each having a different purpose and function. The computer inside a bank ATM is programmed to spit out money after specific buttons are pressed. The computer at the drive thru car wash is programmed to open and close a set of valves and pumps when a command is entered. The computer on your television is programmed to switch to a different channel when you hit a button on the remote. You get the point. They are all computers, but they all have a different purpose and function. They each have a different operating system.

Our mind is very much like the computer systems of this world which we have come to know so well. First, each of these computers must be programmed with information which will then produce a desired result. Second, and most importantly, you cannot take any one of these operating systems and place it into a different computer which has a different purpose or function. It just will not work. This, however, is exactly what we do with the 'program' in our brains when we take on the life of the poser. We attempt to rewrite our program in an effort to make it fit into the false life that we have created which is something that we were not intended or made to be. This just does not work – and therefore our lives do not work either!

Hang with me here – I did say that we needed to learn how to reprogram our computer. Yes, we can reprogram our computer to get more desirable results. The problem with most of us though, is that we rarely endeavor to reprogram or change the output of our computer, we simply change the housing or the environment in which that program operates. We put our program into a different creation, or package, which we come up with on our own and expect the outcome or results to improve. Our program was not created for that life or environment; therefore, it fails every time.

Just like the vast majority of what we see in life, our perspective and our perception on how to correct the problem is flawed. We are looking at the problem with an inadequate awareness. And since our perspective and understanding of any issue is flawed, any attempt that we make at a correction will be proportionately flawed as well.

Almost 90% of what we see and perceive to be happening in our lives every day is misinterpreted or misunderstood. Even though we like to think that we do understand, the actual truth and reality is that there is a whole lot more going on in our lives and in our world than we care to admit to or possess the ability to understand. Try and wrap your mind around that for just a minute......... ninety percent of what goes on in your day-to-day life is not actually what you perceive it to be! On average we are awake for roughly sixteen hours each day. That equates to roughly fourteen and a half hours each day in which we don't have a clue to the actual meaning or purpose of the things that we are experiencing.

Hmmm! That's interesting. We misunderstand or misinterpret 90% of what we see and perceive to be happening. And a few pages back we also found that Psychologists believe that 90% of our thoughts and behaviors come from our subconscious mind. Can the two be related? Is this merely a coincidence? I would think that it's highly likely there is a correlation between the two.

Since we are unable to correctly interpret the happenings in our life, we essentially become packed full of useless, inadequate falsehoods – which we then build our entire lives around.

Does it ever get better? Can we ever truly change for the better? Well, the short answer is yes. However, our perspective (perception) is nothing more, and never greater, than the cumulation of our past experiences. If we are unable to change our perspective and understanding of things, which would then yield a new set of experiences, we will never be more than what we have exposed ourselves to in the past.

My perspective and understanding changed greatly, by the grace of God, on the day that He removed the veil of darkness from my life and allowed me to see His truths.

The Apostle Paul tells us in 2 Corinthians 3:14 (NLT) – *"But the people's minds were hardened, and to this day whenever the old covenant is being read, the same veil covers their minds so they cannot understand the truth. And this veil can be removed only by believing in Christ."*

Paul then goes on to tell us - *"But whenever anyone turns to the Lord, the veil is taken away."* 2 Cor 3:16

All of us live in the darkness, up to some point in our lives at least. The darkness caused by Satan, through the wounds which have been inflicted upon us and are meant to keep us in that darkness. We perceive and come to accept this darkness and these wounds as our reality, and as the only reality that exists. We then refuse to acknowledge or believe in the possibility of any other existence, as again; we are never greater than the cumulation of our past experiences.

We don't believe in God, we don't believe in religion, we don't believe another viewpoint that someone else is trying to share with us, and so on, and so on, and so on.......... simply because we have not experienced it ourselves, in our past, therefore, it must not be real.

Our life is much like that of a dark room. I'm sure that at some point in your life you have found yourself in complete darkness, whether it be a room with no lighting, being outdoors in the country on an overcast night, or maybe when you first wake up in the morning. There is no light. Nothing to illuminate the features around you. You begin to use your hands, reaching for something of familiarity. You lean heavily on your mind, trying to recall all of the objects that you last saw before the darkness. What you are experiencing is called spatial disorientation; having lost all ability to determine your position or relative motion.

The lives we live are very much like our eyes in respect to the darkness. In complete darkness, our eyes adapt by dilating our pupils to capture more light. They activate light-sensitive rod cells in the retina, which detect low light but not color, while cone cells which are used for color become inactive, shifting our vision to black and white. Light-absorbing chemicals like rhodopsin regenerate, allowing us to eventually see shapes and movement over twenty to thirty minutes. Initially, we see nothing, but as those rods activate and rhodopsin reforms, we start to perceive faint shapes, movement, and contrast, often through the use of our peripheral vision.

Our retina's circuitry can become so sensitive that random neural firings create visual 'noise', like faint flashes or patterns, even without light. Our brain's visual cortex generates closed-eye hallucinations (also known as closed-eye visualizations) in the absence of any external input. Our mind basically begins to give us something to see, which is most always just noise or faint impressions which cannot be interpreted.[2]

Any guesses on which part of the mind (conscious or subconscious) controls our vision? Yep, you are correct! A significant portion of our visual processing is controlled by our subconscious mind – the part of our brain that controls 90% of what we do without any effort or intention. This understanding helps to explain why it is so easy for our eyes to wander, quickly being grabbed by anything that moves. It also helps in realizing why we struggle to stay focused at times, especially when we are in new surroundings.

Christopher Butler, a graphic designer, wrote a very in-depth article titled *Understanding the Eye-Mind Connection.*[3]

Butler states:

We are mostly unaware of the information our eyes bring in. When our minds wander, they don't stop thinking, and those thoughts form into judgements regardless of how conscious we are of that happening.

In other words, when we first give anything our attention, it is a distraction from what we were focused on before. This is true even when we are looking for that thing. And that is where judgement comes in. We scan that thing and our mind asks, "is this the thing I'm looking for?" and often answers "yes" or "no" before we are even conscious of it.

Our entire body works like that. Most physical function is autonomous, which is astounding when you stop to ponder it. You don't have to consciously tell your eyes to blink, your lungs to breathe, your throat to swallow, your legs to hold you up, or your fingertips to feel. Virtually every cell of your body does its thing without being micromanaged by the brain. But our experience of every single one of the functions those cells perform does rely upon the brain. Being conscious — being aware — of what your body is doing, then, is relatively rare.

We scan the world, take in information, make judgements about it, and even take action without consciously thinking about it. So the order of our information — how we structure it, format it, align visual anchor points to it, abstract it pictorially, edit and simplify it, and even style it all matter to how the eye portrays it to the mind.[3]

This is the case with our existence as well. We are living in darkness, unable to see what actually exists and what true reality is. Therefore, our mind creates images and scenarios for us that we are able to comprehend. Our mind creates a new reality for us based off of our understanding of our past experiences, and it does so most often without us even being aware that it is happening.

God tells us in Jeremiah 33:3 – *"Call to me and I will answer you and tell you great and unsearchable things you do not know."*

Once that veil of darkness is removed, we begin to see what reality truly is. We begin to see the truth, the way, and the light, which had always been right in front of us before, which we had perceived to be something that was not real.

Being Naked

Now that we have an awareness of the wounds which establish the life of the poser, we are better equipped to understand why and how these wounds have the ability to transform our entire existence into something different than who we are.

Once again, we can go all the way back to the beginning of this world, and the Garden of Eden. The place where that very first attack occurred.

God had just created the world, along with Adam and Eve, who lived in the Garden of Eden. Eden was a perfect, sinless existence, providing for their every need. God had only one rule for Adam and Eve – *"You are not to eat from the Tree of Knowledge and Power!"* That one tree in the middle of the garden. They had been given the whole world, except for that one tree.

In walks, or slithers, Lucifer. It was actually a serpent, a snake, and most certainly being controlled by Lucifer, or Satan, as he and his fallen angels were the only sin in the heavens and on earth.

The serpent could actually talk, and deceived Eve in to believing that she could eat from that one tree and then made her question what God had really said and meant. Satan deceived Eve in to believing that if she did eat from that tree, she would know all that God knows (Does this sound familiar with your life?).

Although God had already given Adam and Eve everything in the whole world, except for that one tree, they wanted more – just as we do today. Eve fell prey to the deception and the lies of Satan and ate that apple from the tree and then gave some to Adam who was nearby. At this point, the actions of Adam and Eve had allowed an opening for sin to enter mankind, which then began the never-ending war. Sin was now an inherent part of mankind and would be so for all who lived in this world. Soon after, God placed punishment for the sin upon the man and woman, as well as the serpent. God had originally given reign over all the world to mankind. As a consequence for his sin, man lost that reign when God gave Lucifer, or Satan, reign over all of the earth........ for the time being.

This sin is not the *'why and how'* of the poser's life, however. It is what transpires next in the story of Adam and Eve that fuels the intentions of the poser.

As part of their punishment, God evicted Adam & Eve from the Garden of Eden. Prior to their eviction, Adam and Eve would spend most of their day walking with and talking to God. After the attack by Satan, with the sin that had now entered their lives, Adam and Eve now began to see things with a different perspective, just as we do. Their wound, just as ours does, changed their view of what reality truly was.

Genesis 3:9-11 is where it all begins. After their eviction, God was going through the garden looking for Adam. Adam and Eve hid among the trees. God then called out to Adam, who replies *"I heard you in the garden, so I hid. I was afraid because I was naked."* Then God asked, *"Who told you that you were naked?"*

We could dive in to so many different discussions on what these verses unfold, but for now we will just focus on Adam being afraid. Adam had eaten the apple from the forbidden tree and had suddenly become aware that he was naked. And now he was afraid, or should we say ashamed of his nakedness. However, Adam had been naked his entire life, and it had never been a concern to him before. So why now?

When Adam ate the apple, sin and Satan entered mankind. Adam did not know what sin was before this time. And as is always the case with Satan, first comes the lies and deceptions that lead us to sin, and then he pours on the guilt and the shame to make us feel bad about what we have done, and unworthy of being close to God. Adam now felt that shame and for the first time in his life he felt that he had to hide from God out of that shame.

We react in this same manner when we are trying to be something other than our true selves. We are ashamed of our true selves, and therefore we always attempt to blend into whatever situation we find ourselves in, portraying an image of something that we are not. We are afraid of being exposed for who we truly are. We are fakes, we are phonies, we are all frauds. And we do so because we are ashamed of who we truly are, and what others may think of us if we show our true selves. We allow the world and mankind to shape and mold the person that we should be all in an effort to fit in and be accepted. All to receive that affirmation and validation that we so desperately seek and crave. All so that we may be desired.

We have also been deceived into believing that we can acquire this acceptance from other people as well as the world, and in that acceptance we will now be complete.

This is where the life of the poser begins. Shame! Our own personal perception and belief that we are unworthy and not good enough. That the person who we are and the qualities that we have are not desirable. The attacks and the wounds are just a tool used to make us feel inadequate and damaged.

Once we possess that view, that perception, of being damaged and inadequate, Satan bombards us with the guilt and shame that our life will never amount to anything worthy by being the person that we are. And since we cannot quench or dispose of that innate desire that we were made with, we change who and what we are in a necessitating attempt to satisfy that desire.

"For the time will come when people will not put up with sound doctrine. Instead, to suit their own desires, they will gather around them a great number of teachers to say what their itching ears want to hear. They will turn their ears away from the truth and turn aside to myths." 2 Timothy 4:3-4

Chapter 7

Shame

Let's recap the first six chapters to ensure that we understand the primary components involved in establishing the life of the poser. And let's not forget – we are all posers to one degree or another.

- We were created with the innate quality of desire. Always seeking, always wanting, always looking for something or someone else. We were given this desire so that we may want, seek, and look for God. Over time, with the wounds that we receive, we begin to misunderstand that desire as well.

- Spiritual warfare is real and is a constant in our lives and the world which we live in. The enemy, Satan, seeks to derail any plans or direction that God intends for our lives and does so by inflicting wounds upon us from a very young age.

- These wounds cause us to alter our perspective of reality, mostly out of self-preservation, which then leaves us with a flawed perception of all things.

- This flawed perception then begins to form our new reality with an understanding that is contrary to what is actually happening.

- These attacks by Satan most always hit us in our most vulnerable places, where it will hurt the most, in the areas of our heart and soul that mean the most to us.

- Once Satan has inflicted these wounds, he then hits us with the blame and shame. It is our fault that this happened or that things are this way, and we should feel terrible about it.

This blame and shame is where the life of the poser emerges and begins to flourish. Just like all of the other lies and deceptions that Satan has piled upon us, we accept and believe that the wounds we have received were brought about by something that we did. It was our fault. It was by our doing. And if we would have just done something differently, or acted in a different manner, the wound would not have happened.

Since we are always trying to learn and adapt, this shame and guilt move us to modify who we are in an attempt to better ourselves so that we do not make those perceived mistakes again, and so that we don't have to endure the pain associated with those mistakes again. We then begin the transformation of who and what we are, again, not so much because of the wound, but more so as a result of the guilt and shame which we have allowed ourselves to accept with that wound.

What is Shame?

According to Arlin Cuncic, author of The Anxiety Workbook[1]:

Shame is a feeling of embarrassment or humiliation that arises from the perception of having done something dishonorable, immoral, or improper. People who experience shame usually try to hide the thing they feel ashamed of. When shame is chronic, it can involve the feeling that you are fundamentally flawed. Shame can often be hard to identify in oneself.

While shame is a negative emotion, its origins play a part in our survival as a species.[2]

Cuncic goes on to state: *Since we want to be accepted, shame is an evolutionary tool that keeps us all in check.*[2]

The key takeaway from her statement is that shame is a feeling. A feeling that arises from our perception, or the way in which we see something to be. We have already learned that the vast majority of what we see playing out in our lives every day is not fully what it appears to be. So, it would only be reasonable to conclude that the vast majority of what we perceive may be incorrect as well. Therefore, we could surmise that those feelings of embarrassment and shame that we inflict upon ourselves from these faulty perceptions are unfounded and without reason.

There are four main types of shame according to modern day psychologists: Existential shame, Situational shame, Class shame, and Narcissistic shame.

- Existential shame stems from a fundamental sense of inadequacy or unworthiness, often rooted in early childhood experiences. It is a pervasive feeling that one is inherently flawed or not good enough.

- Situational shame is triggered by specific events or situations that cause a person to feel embarrassed, humiliated, or exposed. Examples such as being caught in a lie, making a public mistake, or experiencing a social blunder.

- Class shame is related to social class and socioeconomic status. It involves feeling ashamed of one's background, financial situation, or social standing.

- Narcissistic shame is associated with having a fragile ego or a deep-seated fear of being exposed as flawed or imperfect. It often leads to defensive behaviors like grandiosity, perfectionism, or a tendency to blame others.

Existential shame

As we discussed in Chapter 5, many of our wounds come at an early childhood age. And once those wounds are inflicted, the shame is quick to follow. From a very young age we begin to feel inadequate, unworthy, and that who and what we are as a person is not good enough. We then begin to interpret everything in our existence with this faulty view. The view that we will never amount to anything worthy. The perspective that we will always be less than everyone else. The belief that we will never be accepted as we are because we feel fundamentally damaged and broken.

Situational shame

It is probably safe to say that we have all experienced situational shame at one point or another in our lives. None of us are perfect. Therefore, we make mistakes and do things we quickly regret and wish we could take back. Situational shame most always occurs in a group setting, or when many others are around to witness our little screw-up. And since we are always seeking affirmation and validation from others, as we desire to be accepted, the embarrassment and shame come upon us quickly after our perceived failure.

Class shame

This type of shame is instilled upon us at a young age as well. One of the biggest lessons forced upon us in our school systems relates to class. No, not the classroom, the social class. In our schools, we commonly refer to it as cliques or groups of different people. In my Junior and Senior High school, the big three were the Jocks, the Preppies, and the Stoners. We also had the Nerds, the Asians, the Eggheads, and the Losers. It doesn't matter what you call them though; it's all separation and division in an attempt to make others feel as though they are less than you are. And just a side note – separation and division is another major tactic used by Satan. God believes in unity and multiplication.

The irony of the matter though, is that each group desired and perceived themselves to be better than the other groups, while on an individual level each member of every group feels some level of inadequacy in who they are. Regardless of how we label a group or class, almost all of us attempt to portray a social status that exceeds our emotional status – simply to keep others down so that we may not be the only ones stuck in a miserable existence.

Narcissistic shame

A narcissist is: *an extremely self-centered person who has an exaggerated sense of self-importance.*[3] Narcissists possess a false sense of superiority and entitlement over others, as well as a constant need for praise and admiration from others. Narcissists also have difficulty understanding and relating to the feelings of others, leading them to be unsympathetic with a disregard for others.

While the 'Full-blown poser' has many of the same tendencies as the narcissist, being a 'Full-blown poser' does not instinctively make one a narcissist.

These four categories of shame are again what psychologists refer to as the 'main' types. There are many others which we experience every day, and new labels and subtypes are routinely being created as well. Regardless of the type that has touched and affected one's life, the feeling of inadequacy received from that shame is the fuel that drives one to alter their existence in the hope of never having to endure that shame again.

Each different variation of shame, along with the way in which that shame is perceived, creates a different version of the poser. With different individuals, each carrying a different perspective, each coming from a different environment, and each retaining different wounds – the variations of the poser are infinite.

With shame comes condemnation. Condemnation is defined as: *the act of declaring something awful or evil.*[4]

Condemnation

- In shame we condemn ourselves for being the person we are.

- Shame is a dimension of condemnation that reaches into the deepest levels of our soul.

- It touches our identity and causes self rejection.

- We feel ourselves to be a failure for just being the person we are.

- We wish to be someone else, but of course we cannot.

- We feel trapped, and our life is made hopeless.

- Therefore, we attempt to become something other than who we truly are.

My Shame

As we discussed in earlier chapters, the war is ongoing. It does not stop. Therefore, it is not just that one initial wound that we receive which transforms our lives, it is a multitude of wounds occurring over the course of our entire life. The attacks continue, the wounds deepen, the shame continues to mount, and we never stop reworking who we are in an effort to simply survive, avoid the pain, and eliminate any shame.

I have spent numerous years in all four of the main types of shame listed above, each at varying stages of my life, and each brought on by a different wound and the way in which I perceived that wound to affect me. And while not every poser will face every type of shame, it is not an uncommon occurrence.

From a very young age, my life was much less than what most people would consider as desirable. My father had left, my mother was never around, and my older brother and I were running the streets doing whatever we pleased. Most kids grow up receiving at least a basic level of guidance and direction from their parents. Teachings such as how to interact with others, communicate with others, and follow some sense of moral code. Training on how to handle yourself in certain situations, preparing you for the big ugly world that they will one day release you in to. And if nothing else, even at the most elementary level, they would instruct you on proper self-care and hygiene.

My brother and I had none of that. We had 'the streets'. We had to learn on our own, and we had to learn from what we saw and experienced on those streets. Don't get me wrong. 'The streets' will surely teach you countless things, many of which I believe should be taught to our younger generations. However, 'the streets' don't care who you are, and 'the streets' don't care if you are alive tomorrow or not. 'The streets' teach all of us different things, mostly because we

all see and perceive things differently. There is one thing that 'the streets'
teach everyone though – how to survive!

One of my favorite bands growing up was *Triumph*, a three-man rock
band from Canada. In the early 1980's, Triumph released their sixth album
titled *Never Surrender*. The lyrics for the title track offered a fair perspective of life on the streets stating:

Out in the streets inspiration comes hard
The joker in the deck keeps handin' me his card
Smilin' friendly he takes me in
Then breaks my back in a game I can't win
Jivin', hustiln', what's it all about?
Everybody always wants the easy way out
Thirty golden pieces for the Judas kiss
What's a nice boy doin' in a place like this?[5]

People who live the street life are much like piranhas. They will chew you
up and spit you out without even giving it a second thought. Life is about
survival on the streets, and it becomes every man/woman for themselves.
These people are living that life as they have no other options. They have
nowhere else to go. They most always have very few possessions, if any, and
are scratching and clawing for whatever they can get in life. And if you
happen to be what stands between them and something that they perceive
of value, well, I'm sorry my friend, you don't stand much of a chance.

My brother and I learned really quick to adapt and survive. More so
myself than my brother although, as it was not long before he befriended
the neighborhood drug dealer whom everyone knew as suicide Mike. Mike
happened to have his own house, which my brother then moved into. I was
on my own, once again, trying to just survive.

The streets offer up countless different situations and opportunities at any given moment. The choices are difficult, and many times they must be made quickly. Make the wrong choice, put yourself in the wrong situation, and it could be the last choice that you ever make. To survive on the streets, one must learn the ability to adapt, or modify who you are, on the fly. You have to possess the ability to change the person that you were just five minutes ago into something that is completely different, all while correctly assessing who and what this new person should be like. And even though my life as a poser began many years before, unbeknownst to me, this is where my crash course would begin, and where I would also receive my master's degree.

As the streets are ruthless and unforgiving, one almost never receives praise or validation for anything they may have accomplished. It is every man/woman for themselves, with no one else to lift you up or support you as this would only mean less for themselves. Instead, the streets are quick to induce those wounds and scars, and eager to bombard you with shame just to keep you one rung lower on the ladder than everyone else.

Many of my wounds, and a good portion of the shame in my life was obtained during this period. And since I did not have any other influence on my life, one which may lend a positive perspective, these views and beliefs became my reality. It was all I knew. It was my world, and the only world which I believed to exist. Day after day, more and more, I would buy into the lies, the deceptions, and the shame that was being force fed to me.

> *I could have been the poster child for shame, and I am sure that many of you feel that way as well. This feeling, this place, is exactly where Satan wants us to remain and he is doing everything he can to make sure that we spend our lives there.*

The wounds which had brought on the shame in my life led me to believe and accept that I was less than everyone else. To have a perspective that the lives of others outside of my world were so perfect and organized, while my life was nothing that could ever be desired. I wanted nothing more than to escape this nightmare that I lived in but did not see how that would ever be possible as I would never be accepted or amount to anything worthy. Those other people would never allow me into their world as I had nothing to offer. They would never support me or encourage me as damaged and broken as I was. And I would never be able to fit in as I was a degenerate with no family and a disastrous past.

Little did I know then that everyone else's life was just as deplorable as mine, they had just learned how to masquerade it as something other than it was.

Agreements

Much of what leads us into our life as a poser is the agreements that we make. Things that we buy into. Things that we begin to accept, believe, and agree with. We've learned that the wounds which have been inflicted upon us cause us to see things with a different perspective, most notably ourselves. We then begin to see ourselves and our lives as being far less than adequate or desirable. This erroneous perception of ourselves leads us to the shame which we then immerse ourselves in. The shame then causes us to commence the creation of our poser persona so that we may distance ourselves as far as possible from that embarrassing, undesirable slug that we once were.

Hold on a minute.......... Aren't we supposed to have 'free will'?

Yes, it is true, we do have free will. Remember Chapter 3? God gave every one of us that free will. The freedom to make our own choices.

Well then, if we can make our own choices, don't we have the ability to choose NOT to be led into the poser life?

We'll dive into the topic of choices later in Chapter 15. For now, we'll just focus on the agreements we make, many of which we may not even realize.

What is an agreement? Well, in regard to our lives, it is anything that we align ourselves with, accept as being true, allow to go on, or believe as being a part of who we are. Agreements can be either beneficial or harmful, depending on what it is that we are agreeing to.

Relating to the life of the poser, many of our agreements come right after our wounds are inflicted, and right before the shame is piled on. Satan hits us with his attack, causing some form of pain in our life, and then plants the accusations and lies into our minds. The accusations and lies are meant to change our perspective, causing us to then view matters differently, eventually leading us down a different road with a perspective that now sees all things incorrectly.

This is a crucial moment in any attack. The moment when we are faced with the choice to either agree with the BS that Satan is trying to get us to buy into or stomp it out immediately and recognize the lies and deceptions for what they are. Unfortunately, all of us have fallen victim to the lies and all of us have made agreements with Satan and the darkness in these moments of the attack.

It is in these agreements, when we chose to align ourselves with the lies that are being fed to us, that we choose to believe in something other than who we are and choose to listen to and follow something or someone other than our Creator. It is these agreements which keep us living the life of the poser and keep us living in darkness and bondage.

These agreements are most always simple in nature, which is the way Satan works, keeping the decisive tactics from becoming obvious. We must learn to realize the agreements that we have made, and then break those agreements, for us to return to the life that we were created to live.

Listed below are just a few general agreements that we commonly align ourselves with:

- I am no good and will never amount to anything special.
- I have a crappy life and those are just the cards that I was dealt.
- Bad things happen to me all the time.
- Nothing good ever happens in my life.
- I don't deserve to be loved so it is no surprise that I don't have any friends.
- I am not very good at anything, so why even try.
- I can't rely on other people to be there when I need them.
- Other people only care about themselves. To protect myself from being hurt again I'm going to trust no one.
- I can't let others see the true me – the me that is shameful and embarrassing. And one of my favorites -
- Here we go again!

These are just a few, but I think you get the point. These agreements are endless and come at us all day long, every day. They are Satan's way of trying to get us to agree with something other than the truth, and to align us with his plans and goals for our life. We need to break these agreements that we have made in the past and then learn to recognize them when they confront us moving forward so that we don't allow ourselves to enter into them again.

By the time we reach Chapter 20, we'll explore how to break the agreements we've made in the past.

All of us are dealing with shame. It is simply a part of the bigger picture of life which we are unable to see. It is part of the ongoing war, and a weapon that our enemy utilizes to keep us wounded and keep us out of the fight. While we are living in this shame, we feel as if there is no hope. We feel as if it will never end and there is no way out. We then accept and believe that this is who we truly are.

The truth of the matter is that we are so much more than this. And while we may not allow ourselves to believe it at first, we must keep telling ourselves this truth every day. We must replace the lies and deceptions that we have come to accept and believe with the truths, which will then become our new beliefs.

You do matter! You are important! And you are worthy – worthy of the entire world!

Now – stop listening to Satan and start living in the promises of the one who made us, our Father!

"For God did not give us a spirit of fear. He gave us a spirit of power and of love and of a good mind." 2 Timothy 1:7 NLV

Chapter 8

What Drives Us?

So far, we have come to understand the primary catalysts which trigger our transformation into the life of a poser, as well as the reasoning behind the poser's existence. By now, you are hopefully beginning to detect a bit of the poser in you. If not, don't pat yourself on the back just yet, as we will now bring our discussion a bit closer to home, making my original statement that we are all posers clear and evident.

The Change

We have learned that the wounds and scars we receive leave us shattered and broken, pushing us into a state of defense, or self-preservation. We have also come to see that while we are in this state, shame is layered upon us with the intent of keeping us in this position, and to keep us from fighting back. This state of shame is a form of bondage, or slavery. Once we allow ourselves to buy into that shame, we are essentially allowing that shame (and Satan) to dictate our actions, our thoughts, our lives, and the direction of our lives. We then become submissive to that shame, empowering it to mold and shape who and what we are and become.

Once again, this is Satan's goal – to take us out of the fight, and to keep us out of the fight.

In this state of self-preservation, we have only two choices for moving forward.:

Our first option would be to get back up and brush ourselves off, trying to recall the strong, confident warrior and person who we are, and get back into the fight. Making this choice, however, means opening ourselves up and accepting the likelihood of getting hurt once again. Most often, however, that hurt, and the pain and suffering which accompany it, is something which we cannot see ourselves surviving yet another time.

Our mind and our subconscious thought are hard-wired for self-preservation, or survival. They are also wired to perform tasks and functions with as much efficiency as possible, allowing us to conserve energy – or, to take the easy way out, the path of least resistance. Therefore, each and every one of us, with the very rare exception, will always choose the second option.

Our second option would be to change who we are, while attempting to suppress and ignore the wounds which we have received. This, my friends, is exactly what we do and what we have done. While many of us won't recall the where, when or why – we chose this option for the first time many years ago when we opened the door to our new life as a poser.

In doing so, we allow those wounds to define us and who we are. We are then only able to see ourselves as broken, damaged, worthless and unworthy, which by the way is solely OUR perception of the matter, and we no longer like or care for the person that we are. We then see it as a necessity to change who we are, believing that if we can become something or someone else, those wounds will no longer be a part of who we are, thus enabling us to once again pursue a happy and joyful life.

With our flawed perception and understanding, we bury those wounds deep inside our soul, swearing to never face them again. We then begin to transform into someone or something which we believe others will perceive as a better version of us. Yet again, we are attempting to create something new through the use of our highly impaired perception.

Any resulting change will ultimately be more so defective than the original as it was created with a flawed understanding that was far from perfect. Furthermore, those wounds which we chose to conceal, they are still there. And regardless of how hard we may try; they will not stay buried forever. Eventually, something will bring them to the surface, and we will have to face them one way or another.

It's no coincidence that this tendency to change has become a pattern in nearly every aspect of our lives today. From our appliances to our smart phones, T.V.'s, cars, careers, and even our relationships. Once anything in our life starts performing in a manner other than what we expect, we perceive it as being damaged and immediately begin to look for a replacement. We are no longer willing to invest our time or confidence in anyone or anything – including ourselves.

We, as a society, haven't always carried this tendency though. It seems to have come on within the last forty years or so. Which would lead one to an assumption that it has been learned and therefore taught at some level. Well, I am no scholar by any means, but I do not recall any instruction at any level that taught us to:

- spend all of our hard-earned money on the things that we need – and then get rid of those things as quickly as possible.

- spend years getting a degree so that we may obtain a good paying job – and at the first sign of adversity, abandon ship.

- spend years trying to find a good relationship – and at the first disagreement, get rid of them.

- Invest in your health, invest in your hygiene, invest in your financial future – but don't waste your time investing in self-belief as you are just damaged goods that won't amount to much anyways.

I do not think any of us could find a college or university that offers such a class. And even if one did, no one would enroll. The degrading attacks on one's psyche are just too obvious. So where must we be learning this, or getting this from? Hmmmm....... slow, subtle attacks on your psyche (soul). A lack of commitment or investment in yourself or anyone else. And the perfectly aged-like-fine-wine puddle of shame that we have been living in.

If it is not glaringly obvious where all of this garbage is coming from, might I recommend going back to Chapter 1 and starting over from the beginning of the book.

The Drive

Aside from the wounds and shame that we live in, which have instigated the transformation in our lives, the grown-up or adult poser evolves into something much more complex. It is no longer a matter of trying to hide from those wounds or the shame, as we have long since forgotten what those wounds are and where we even buried them. The adult poser has spent years in this life, if not decades. The functions and the processes of this poser have become so deeply ingrained that they are purely habitual by now. The adult poser will have successfully reprogrammed their subconscious, that part of our mind which guides 90% of our thoughts and actions – without any conscious effort required.

They are unable see this new version of themselves as anything new at all, however. They only see who they are now, and they wholeheartedly believe that this is who they have always been. They have very little recollection of that past life, if any, as the wounds, the pain, the shame, and the embarrassment of that life have all driven them to distance themselves from it as far as possible.

What the poser does not see, however, is the dichotomy of their new life. This new life, which was formed in an attempt to run and hide from the shame and embarrassment in the old life, will make every effort to disconnect from that old life out of a similar shame and embarrassment.

As the poser matures and the new subconscious thought processes begin to take control, our lives are pretty much on autopilot at this point. As mentioned previously, there are countless variations of the poser, and each will have their own unique traits and tendencies. However, there are three main attributes to the poser life, and at least one of them can be found in every poser, if not all three.

These three qualities drive all of us, in our life as the poser. They are what fuels our day-to-day existence, quickly becoming the framework for everything that we do. Without them our life as a poser would be no more meaningful than that deplorable slug which we chose to abandon so many years ago. Mastering these characteristics becomes a matter of survival for us. Through the world that we live in we are led to believe that employing these three qualities will ensure that we obtain the love, admiration, affirmation, and validation which we inherently desire. Therefore, we are willing to go to great lengths and do almost anything to possess them.

Performance

Appearance

Status

Performance

How this poser performs, in any aspect or manner, becomes paramount in their perception of their own self-worth. This poser will build their entire life around their performance, perceiving that their effort and output is what will gain the attentions and affirmations of others. And when this poser is unable to realize the desired responses through their efforts, they will only increase the level of performance, pushing themselves to perform (work) harder, longer, and faster.

This poser sees the performance trait as a life-or-death issue. It is something that we must do for our survival. To us, there is no other option. And for that reason, the poser stuck in this mentality is willing to push themselves to the point of self-destruction, most always ending in a state of emotional, mental and physical exhaustion.

The performance trait is driven by a fear of inadequacy – never being enough or never being good enough.

Appearance

Comprehensively, the life of any poser is modeled around how we believe others see or perceive us. Our appearance, or the person that we appear to be, is why we became something different than we once were. We wanted others to see something other than who we truly were, as we had perceived that our old self would never be good enough.

For many of us posers though, it is all about the look. The outward appearance, the aesthetics. The image that we portray of our new selves and the so-called life that we are supposedly living. To us, it does not matter so much that our true life behind closed doors may be monotonous, boring, and less than desirable. What matters is the image of our life that we convey to everyone else. We simply want everyone else to desire what we supposedly have. We want others to look at us. We want others to be jealous and envious. We want others to wish they had the life that we claim to have.

This poser trait has become commonplace in our society today with the explosion of social media. Our world has made it incredibly easy for one to post a snapshot of their life for everyone else to drool over, causing others to be jealous and envious of the perfect life that someone else has. And with the flawed perspective that we all have, everyone viewing that picture now believes that this one image of one moment in time is representative of what that other person's entire life looks like.

Unfortunately, the show does not stop there for this poser. At some point they do have to step outside of those closed doors. The image that they feel the need to present to others has to be just as ostentatious. In their mind, it is a must that they have the finest and latest fashions, drive the most expensive luxury cars, and be seen doing the things that only the upper class and elites would do. This poser will spare no expense, eventually maxing out the limits on every credit card they have, just to portray an appearance that would be desired by others.

Most posers that possess the appearance trait have a much deeper stigma, however. While the embellishments they have added to their life and their person may seem appealing and desirable to others, they are insufficient at quenching this poser's craving for admiration and desire. Giving in and giving up is not an option for this poser either. Regardless of how ridiculous the chosen method may seem to others, they will continue in their efforts as any conceivable idea quickly becomes justifiable in their mind through their past wounds and is then perceived as a way to obtain that validation which they so greatly desire.

The appearance trait can also lead this poser into modifications of their body – cosmetic surgery. The superficial adornments which they have added to their life are not sufficient, thus leaving them feeling inadequate, less than desirable, and even flawed or faulty in one way or another. For some it is a one-time simple procedure to enhance a certain feature of their body that they perceive to be holding them back. For others it can be multiple procedures, changing several different aspects of their appearance. A rare few will even go to the extent of having a procedure every year until they reach a desired look – that of a completely new person.

The sad part of this poser's life – as is the case with most all posers – is that they are the only ones who see themselves as they do, that of being flawed and undesirable.

This poser will go to great lengths to create an image of a life most people would envy. The reality of this poser is that the person who they truly are is dying on the inside as they give away every bit of their soul in a futile attempt to impress and please others.

The appearance trait is driven by a fear of abandonment and/or rejection.

Status

I think we all carry a little bit of the status trait within us. We are all posers, and all posers possess a fear of inadequacy for one reason or another. We have all been hurt. We have all been let down or disappointed. We have all been passed over in one way or another. And we have all been told at one time or another, directly or indirectly, that we are not good enough.

In our transformation to the poser life, we subconsciously rewrite the playbook for our lives. And to avoid the pain of that rejection and inadequacy, we vow to seek and obtain a higher level of status in this world. Our new perception is that this elevated status will either give us more power and control, or make others look up to us and desire to be in our presence.

It is of no significance if that status should be real or not, it only matters to this poser how it is perceived. This trait is commonly found within the narcissist discussed in the previous chapter.

The status trait is driven by a fear of not being in control – or being able to determine the outcome of our own lives.

These three qualities become ingrained in the poser through two sources. The first, which we discussed in Chapter 5, is the seed that is initially planted with the lies and deceptions that alter our perception of matters. That seed is then fully fueled by the world and the society which we live in, constantly pushing us and teaching us that we must perform a certain way, appear a certain way, and live up to a certain standard.

Generally speaking, male posers will more than likely be pushed to produce, perform, work, and provide effort in what they do. Female posers will more than likely be pushed into looking a certain way, acting a certain way, and dressing a certain way.

Fears

Fears keep us locked in the bondage of Satan, never willing to step up and take a risk or do something daring as we are afraid of failure and/or the embarrassment/shame that they would bring upon us. It keeps us simply in a state of trying to just fit in, following what everyone else wants and believes. It keeps us chasing after the world, the things in this world, and everyone else in this world. It keeps us pretending to be something or someone other than who we were truly created to be, something or someone that will never amount to anything of value or meaning, even if it were possible to one day finally receive the love, respect, admiration, and acknowledgment that we so desire.

Fear keeps us from ever becoming the best that we can be and realizing our true potential. What we are actually afraid of is how other people may judge us or see us if we fail. It is not that we are afraid to try; it is that the pain, the rejection, and the perception of being less than others if we do not succeed is more than we can bear.

We spend our entire lives seeking the approval, validation, and acknowledgment of others. We are willing to completely change who we are as a person in hopes that others may like us, desire us, and want to be around us.

Just take a look at any of our societies today. Every one of us still has that innate desire, whether we choose to acknowledge it or not. We spend our entire lives seeking, chasing, and looking for that next big thrill or adventure. The next rush, the next high, the next uplifting moment to make us feel good about ourselves and provide us a moment of joy.

For many of us this leads to affairs, prostitutes, and sexual encounters with anyone and everyone that we can as we so desperately need the attention of other people. For countless others who have already experienced the eventual rejection of people one too many times, it is often drugs, alcohol, or some impersonal activity that becomes their new pleasure and pursuit.

The flawed perspective of our self-image is the driving factor which leads us to this new life, and the desired validation from others. However, it is this same flawed perspective that does not allow us to see that what we are chasing after comes from others whose perspective is just as flawed and distorted as ours.

We are all moved and motivated by one simple thought in everything that we do. What we do. What we say. How we dress. How we act, react, and interact with others. And how we mold and shape the direction of our lives.

That one simple thought that drives each and every one of us, and is a cornerstone in the life of the poser –

"What will other people think?"

"Do not conform to the pattern of this world, but be transformed by the renewing of your mind. Then you will be able to test and approve what God's will is—his good, pleasing and perfect will." Romans 12:2

Chapter 9

A Poser I Am

I've mentioned it plenty of times already– We are all posers. Nevertheless, I have a feeling that some of you might still not agree with this statement. Unfortunate as that may be, I realize that in spite of my efforts to bring awareness to this truth, some will be so deeply rooted in the self-life that it will not be possible for them to see what reality actually is.

As I've also mentioned, I was the King of Posers and had mastered the self-life. I too had been held captive by this mentality and skewed perspective. Thankfully, the veil of darkness was removed from my life allowing me to see what reality truly was. Once I began to see the truth, it completely blew me away. I then began to picture the countless others that were living life just as I was and quickly realized they needed to know these truths and this reality as well and be made aware of the deception which they had fallen prey to. This was not something that I could keep to myself. It had to be shared. People like me had to know that the life we were living was nothing but a lie designed to keep us from living life to its fullest.

The self-life, along with our mentality of simply trying to survive, leads us to hold little regard for others, if any. Just take a quick look around as you go about your day. It is every man, woman, and child for themselves. It truly is a fight when we venture outside of our homes – and for some of us, even more so inside our homes. But yet again, we refuse to accept the fact that spiritual warfare is a real thing and that it is playing out in our lives every single day.

C'mon people! Let's be honest with ourselves. Do you really think that all there is to life is some sixty, seventy, eighty years of chaos and struggle, sprinkled with the occasional attempt to grab some happiness and joy – and then it's all over? Do you really believe this is all we were created for? There has to be more. There has to be a greater purpose for our lives. And I would think that even the bleakest of us would hope so as well.

This utter blindness which we all experience at some point makes us question and doubt everything and everyone around us. This too is by design. Its intention – separation and division. Without diving in too deeply – God's plan is union, unity, and harmony, in all people and all things. God created us to need and want others in our lives. Satan wants to thwart God's plans. Therefore, Satan is fighting against God's plan every single day. And if you have any knowledge or awareness of war tactics, one strategy that is always utilized is to divide and conquer, or separation and division.

The Merriam-Webster dictionary defines the idiom *divide and conquer* as:
to make a group of people disagree and fight with one another so that they will not join together against one[1]

When Satan can separate us, whether it be by race, color, creed, origin, gender, or whatever means – and then bring us to fight amongst each other, he has already won the battle. He has achieved his goal of thwarting God's plan. Now, take a look at your life, and your world. Then, in all honesty, try to tell yourself that this IS NOT happening everywhere you go!

Propensities

Just as some of you may have difficulty swallowing the fact that we actually do play an important role in this day-to-day war, the ignorance placed upon us by Satan also makes it extremely challenging to accept that we are all posers. Again, this is not an insult on your intelligence or one's way of life, but merely an endeavor to bring awareness to the false reality that we all have been forced to buy into, and that an alternative does exist, a true reality which is available to each and every one of us.

Let me reiterate what was said in Chapter 3 – *When we are dealing with something about which we are ignorant, we must be slow to criticize just because we are uncomfortable with some of the things that accompany what we don't know. Ignorance is not grounds for rejection.*

The word propensity is defined as: *an intense natural inclination or practice.*[2] It is a tendency, or an established pattern of behavior, with the key word being 'established'. It has been established into our subconscious thought, requiring little or no effort on our part to bring about. It has therefore become a habit or routine which has been so normalized by us that it just happens automatically.

The relative propensities, or natural tendencies, to the life of a poser were formed and ingrained into our subconscious as a result of our flawed perception, and the wounds which we received. They are in a sense our Plan B. They are the protective mechanisms which keep us from placing ourselves into a specific situation or environment similar to that of where and when our wounds occurred, preventing us from being hurt yet again.

As they are utilized for our protection, or so we believe, they become wired to our survival instinct and therefore automatically override our conscious thought for the purpose of our self-preservation. These propensities now shape who and what we become and will do so no matter what the cost to avoid facing the trauma of our past. They become who we are, and we become what they say we are.

They become our narrative for life, or the reasoning and justification for everything that we do.

At this point, you still may be pondering how it is possible, and even plausible, that every one of us could be a poser. The difficulty in this contemplation lies within our perspective. As we discussed in a previous chapter – our perspective (perception) is nothing more, and never greater, than the cumulation of our past experiences. We possess a very limited view of the so-called 'big picture'. Our perspective, which we apply to all things, has been solidified through our understanding of the incredibly small part of the world which we exist in – our surroundings. We then apply this very limited perspective or understanding to all things. And when we apply that limited perspective to matters which are greater than our surroundings, well, the results become a bit blurry. One size does not fit all, and one perspective cannot be applied to all matters that exist.

I am sure that all of us can recall the COVID-19 pandemic (Coronavirus Disease of 2019). A simple little virus that began with one person and ended up taking the lives of thousands. It began in 2019 and became a full blown, worldwide pandemic by early 2020. It seemed like the entire world shut down and nobody knew what they should or should not do. Almost everyone panicked due to a fear of the unknown. That survival instinct that we have kicked in again, and we did whatever we had to do to make sure we survived – no matter how absurd or foolish it may have seemed. The world was sent into chaos with lockdowns, travel bans, food rationing, and government forced vaccinations. The information and propaganda being rampantly spread caused more harm than good as it divided people into two separate groups, giving each one a reason and a cause to hate the other.

We are now in 2025 – five plus years removed from the initial onset of that pandemic. COVID is now a normal and accepted part of our lives throughout the entire world. Yes, we know it is still there. We know it still exists. And we know that it can still take one's life, although not at the severity that it once did. Our world has gone back to functioning as it once did, as normal. Okay, so it's the new norm. Albeit most of us don't even give it a thought anymore as we go about our day.

This is but one example of a global pandemic, which began with one person, and quickly spread to affect our entire world. And five years later it is now all but forgotten. No more chaos. No more panic. No more restrictions. Just another normal part of our everyday lives which we have come to accept and ignore until it affects us directly.

The poser life is no different. It too began with one person. It too spread worldwide. It too became the new norm and what everyone would quickly accept and soon come to ignore. The only difference is that the virus which we contracted as posers has been mutating for thousands of years. It has infected each and every soul on this planet and has done so in a way that we just see as being normal, being reality, being who we are and who we were created to be. We don't take it as seriously as COVID because we can't clearly see the direct connection between the virus and the deaths it causes. However, the number of lives lost to the poser virus will make COVID seem like nothing more than the common cold.

Day-to-Day Life

The day-to-day life of the poser will look no different than that of our own, which is substantiating evidence that we are all posers and that we have come to accept this as the norm or our reality. Typically, there will be no blatantly obvious signs indicating that one is pretending to be something other than their true selves. And they won't stand out from the crowd making themselves quickly noticeable either.

Most always, a poser will not have a deeply held conviction to support, or something that they firmly believe in other than themselves. Many posers, however, will tend to associate themselves with a cause or movement in a vain attempt to bolster their own image. Causes such as saving animals, saving the planet, fighting for world peace, or fighting poverty. While all of these are good causes, very few of us offer true support that genuinely comes from the heart.

Our inability to recognize other posers around us comes about for one reason – We are all posers trying to adapt and fit in with the rest of the world; therefore, others perform and act just as we do. Furthermore, for us to concede that those around us are posers, those people who act and perform in the same manner that we do, would contradict our reluctance to admit that we might be posers ourselves. This is how it is possible for the poser to survive and even flourish in our society. For if we were to bring to light the false beliefs and tendencies of another, we would end up exposing ourselves and thus bring harm to our own way of life. Once again, our survival instinct kicks in, shielding us at all costs, without us even realizing it.

So, what is it that we do in our day-to-day lives that makes us a poser? Below, I have touched on a few common areas of our day-to-day lives, highlighting some examples of the actions which many of us take as the poser. These are not all inclusive of what the poser does but should give you an idea of the life and more than likely help you to see that we are all in fact posers.

Remember, a poser will do what he/she does in order to receive the admiration, affirmation, and validation of others and will most always seek these acknowledgments through their performance, appearance, or status in one way or another.

Work Life

Those of us who are employed – whether it be a job, a career, a gig, or any other form of livelihood – spend a good portion of our time in this environment. Hopefully, it is one which you have a passion for and enjoy, otherwise it can be just plain miserable. Whichever the case may be, the poser in us is overly active in our work environment.

The position that we hold in our employment doesn't enhance or lessen our actions as a poser either. One could be the janitor for a Fortune 500 company or the CEO. One could be self-employed or work with thousands of others. One may work alone or be part of a large team. What we do and who we do it with will have no relevance to our output or performance as a poser. The differences and severity in the performance of each poser in this environment will only be determined by the individual variations and tendencies that each poser has – which have all been formed by that individual's perception and interpretation of their past experiences.

All three of the driving qualities that we discussed in the last chapter (performance, appearance, status) come in to play in the work life of the poser.

We will almost always perform in a certain way or complete certain tasks in such a manner as to get noticed. Even in the smallest of acts which we normally would not perceive as having any benefit, we subconsciously perform in hopes that someone may recognize our efforts. The way in which we arrange our desk and the items that we allow others to see on our desk. The posture that we take when sitting in our office chair. The image that we portray of the employee that we want others to see, which is also not the same image every time. We vary the presentation depending on the value that we perceive could be obtained from those who may notice our efforts.

We also apply these efforts in the projects and tasks that we carry out. Whether we may realize it or not, we perform these tasks and functions with an effort to please or satisfy the expectations of someone else, or what we may perceive those expectations to be. Regardless of whether that other person may be a superior or just another co-worker, we perform in such a manner hoping to gain the acceptance and approval of the other person. We desire to be accepted, acknowledged, and approved of in everything that we do. We crave the validation.

We put forth a similar effort with our appearance as well. How we dress, how we walk, and even how we talk. We begin this attempt at being what others want us to be early in our day by contemplating how others will perceive us if we choose one outfit over another. And once we enter the arena of our work environment, we seemingly take on a new personality; walking, talking, and carrying on in a manner that is inconsistent with our other environments. We alter who we are in all aspects, to become the person that we perceive others want us to be, or to become the person that we want others to see us as.

Much, if not all, of our charade in the work environment is brought about by fear. Fear of losing that job that we have if we do not perform in a certain manner – although, the ways in which we perceive that others want us to perform is once again a perception that only we have. Fear of losing that sale. Fear of losing that client. The fear that we will be seen as not being good enough to meet the other's expectations. Fear of rejection, not fitting in, or not being accepted by the group. The fear that we will sooner than later be seen as the fraud that we are and will lose everything that we have worked so hard to obtain and achieve.

The person in denial of the poser life will quickly attempt to justify every one of the actions mentioned above. Standard replies include stating that this is just the way they are, these are the ways in which they do all things, and this is the way that they have always been. They will insist that their actions are not a front or facade but are of the true person that they have always been. Once again, referring back to Chapter 2 – *Denial is a cognitive process which involves refusing to acknowledge or accept reality, often serving as a defense mechanism against painful feelings or stress.*

Social Life

The efforts that we apply to our social life as a poser differ very little from that of our work life. This should come as no great surprise as the poser is not a complex individual, and our newly created persona was formed out of duress. While our poser persona was created to be someone completely different than the person who we originally were, we must remember that this new person was created using a flawed perspective resulting in the creation of something that is even less than the original was – never more. This new person, the poser, is therefore running and operating on a very limited set of parameters. Those parameters are restricted to, and intently focused on seeking out that admiration, affirmation, and validation in a manner which their faulty perception has led them to believe would be most successful.

The tactics utilized in the social life of the poser will also not vary greatly from other key environments of their life. However, in their social life, the poser amplifies these tactics exponentially. The poser does so as social matters and relationships more directly affect their heart, their soul, and their perceived feeling of self-worth. The validation and affirmation, or the lack thereof, that the poser receives from the social life will always have a much greater impact than that received from any other environment.

In the social life, the poser most always becomes hyper-focused on appearance and status, with less regard for performance. Appearance and status in the life of most all posers is paramount to their existence. They perceive that they must look a certain way and play a certain role to gain the approval of others. Therefore, they are willing to go to great lengths to broadcast an appearance and status that would be worthy and desired by others.

The further amplification of these traits within the poser's social life has reached new heights with the multitude of social media platforms that are available. The poser no longer has to go to great lengths to portray an image of something other than who they truly are. Now, by simply turning on their computer, they can be, or appear to be, anything that they want the world to see.

The meteoric rise in social media platforms, and their usage, is only further confirmation that we all seek the validation and approval of others. This in and of itself should come as no great revelation as the Bible tells us very early on that God did not create us to be alone.

Genesis 2:18 states: *The Lord God said, "It is not good for the man to be alone."*

However, as we have done with everything else through the use of our flawed perspective, we use social media to glorify ourselves. At the same time, whether intentionally or unintentionally, we are bringing others down. It becomes all about us, and how we can make our lives appear so perfect, only for others to be envious and jealous of what we supposedly have. Very rarely do we ever use social media as a platform to encourage or uplift others. As with everything else in the poser life – it is all about "me" and bringing the attention to ourselves.

I am very much aware that many readers will likely disagree with the last paragraph, insisting that they have good intentions on social media and are simply sharing and keeping in touch with others. For this response we must once again refer back to Chapter 3, and the topic of Denial – while remembering that our subconscious mind controls the vast majority of what we do, without any thought or effort from us, and does so in response to our past traumas and wounds.

> **Chapter 3 – Denial**
>
> Denial is a cognitive process which involves refusing to acknowledge or accept reality, even when that reality presents itself with objective facts, often serving as a defense mechanism against painful feelings or stress. This can manifest in the human mind where one consciously or subconsciously avoids or minimizes certain aspects of reality. Denial also involves an attitude of resistance or our refusal to face the truth, which then affects and alters our behavior and interactions.

The performance trait does not come into play in the social life for most of us. However, for posers who have a strong sense of inadequacy and have come to perceive that it is only through exceptional performance that they will ever be accepted, the performance trait will dominate all aspects of their life. The performance driven poser will conversely put forth very little if any effort to glorify their appearance or status. For the performance driven poser, it is all about 'the works'. What they can do, and doing so in a way that is better, faster, and more efficient than others may do it – so that they may be the one receiving the recognition.

This type of poser will always feel the need to 'perform' in their social environment. No matter the relationship, or the length of time that the relationship has persisted, this poser will always make any attempt at building upon or strengthening that relationship through their works or their performance. They will also show any love, desire, or commitment to that relationship through what they do and how they perform as well.

Family/Personal Life

One may think that the poser would abandon their alter persona when being around those that are closest to them. After all, these are people that we have allowed into our inner circle. People that we supposedly trust, having seen our true character, day in and day out. These people, our close friends, family, spouses, and relatives; would surely be able to recognize any variations and would quickly label us as being insincere.

However, discarding the new life that we have chosen is not a possibility for the poser, even if only for a brief period of time. Doing so would require us to return to our original selves, forcing us to face the pain and shame that we could not live with. To the poser, this is not an option. When we made the choice to leave that life behind, we burned all of the bridges and made sure there was no way to turn back. This is true and the new reality even for the periodic poser.

To have a better understanding of how the poser deals with close and intimate relationships, we must first know that it is not possible for one to live in, and therefore act out multiple personalities, for an extended period of time. Whoa! Hold on for just a minute – I know the readers with PhD's have all just thrown their heads back in dismay. Let me clarify that statement by adding that this is true for those with a sound mind, that are unimpaired by a mental illness, drugs, or dementia. And while those with mental impairments may still possess poser tendencies to one extent or the other, our entire discussion refers to those without impairments.

With that being said – Once again – we must first know that it is not possible for one to live in, and therefore act out multiple personalities, for an extended period of time. We are not complex individuals as posers. We are simply putting on a show and playing the part of someone or something that is not our true character. This is also partial reasoning as to why the poser persona is not very complicated. The more complex the new persona is that we need to act out, the greater the chance that we will be unable play it out successfully and soon be caught in our deception. Therefore, we keep it simple, something that is easily rememberable and repeatable.

Furthermore, as this new persona or personas is not who we truly are, we have to constantly work at playing the part and putting on the show. This requires continuous mental effort, which becomes exhausting over time. In an attempt to avert the exhaustion, we switch it up and bring out a new persona when we move into a different environment. The change is still taxing on our mental capacities, however, this change in our thought processes and our persona is in a sense a break. We have the mental ability and strength to keep the charade going for an abbreviated period of time, but any lengthy stay in one persona or environment wears us down and is bound to eventually reveal who we truly are.

Therein lies the difficulty with close family, friends and spouses. These are the people that we spend most of our time with. And yes, just as we are with everyone else in this world, we are posers with these people as well. We are not our true selves. We give in, we settle, we compromise, and we change the person that we are.

Look back to the *Social Life*. The poser amplified their tactics exponentially because social matters and relationships more directly affect their heart, their soul, and their perceived feeling of self-worth. With the 'friends and family plan', this amplification of tactics is on steroids. These are people that we have chosen to be the closest to us in our lives, therefore, they matter the most to us. Any validation, affirmation, or the lack thereof, that the poser receives from this group has what the poser perceives as life-or-death consequences. Posers will do almost anything to keep these people in their lives and to remain in their favor as the validation from these people literally means everything to them.

Sounds a bit overblown, doesn't it? If so, you have likely come to the point of overlooking the little ways in which we give in to these people in our life. Or, as with many of us, you may have reached the point of justification, where it has now become commonplace for you as a poser to justify your surrender to these people with the thought and fear of what may happen if you were to stand your ground – which is more than you care to entertain. But remember – for a person to 'stand their ground', they must first have a set of values or beliefs to stand for, which the poser does not.

With the people in our lives that are closest to us, we routinely compromise who we are and find ourselves willing to sacrifice any values and beliefs so that we don't rock the boat. We do this because of our past. Those wounds that were inflicted upon us, and the perceived trauma that accompanied them. They are still there, deeply buried in our soul, no matter how hard we have tried to suppress them. Our subconscious mind recalls them very clearly and still utilizes them in directing our actions and behaviors every single day. While we may not recall these wounds and the associated pain on a conscious level, our subconscious mind still knows them very well.

And since our subconscious mind is now calling the shots, vividly remembering the pain and anguish that we went through, it steers us away from having to relive that pain ever again. Since this group of people are the most valued to us, our mind automatically recalls that pain from the past any time that we are faced with a decision, choice, or option relating to these people. We immediately jump to the worst-case scenario when we ponder what would happen if we did not give in. Therefore, out of a fear of loss or rejection, we simply avoid any response or action which may bring that possibility to fruition.

We give in, we settle, we compromise, we concede, we accommodate, we submit, we surrender; always changing the person that we are.

We do it with our spouses.

We do it with our friends.

We do it with our relatives.

We eventually do it with anyone and everyone that we have an extended interaction with.

The life as a poser affects all of us, no matter how secure or confident we may consider ourselves to be. All of us were created with desire, specifically the desire to have others love us, want us, and need us. It is this desire which moves us too desperately chase the affirmation, validation, and admiration of others – even others who have no significant meaning or relevance in our lives.

Another paradox for the poser in us awaits as we desperately seek that affirmation, validation, and admiration. As was mentioned earlier in this chapter – the poser is far from being a complex individual. Our primary focus tends to center around satisfying our own desires and needs, so much so that we often struggle to see the bigger picture or consider the potential outcome of a situation.

The paradox that awaits us is in what we have become, and what we now chase after. We are all posers. We are all fake, phony, and inauthentic to some extent. We have all created a different version of ourselves, one that we perceive to be better and more desirable. We have created this new persona to garner the attentions of others, who have become just as fake and phony as we are.

We have completely changed who and what we are so that we may be liked and loved by others. And when we think we have found this in others, what we have found is anything but real or sincere, for everyone else is a poser just as we are.

"This is good, and pleases God our Savior, who wants all people to be saved and to come to a knowledge of the truth." 1 Timothy 2:3-4

Chapter 10

Religion

In the past nine chapters and our discussion of the poser life, several Bible verses have been referenced, and God has been mentioned several times. By now, you may be pondering whether this is a book about life or one about religion. The answer to that question is Yes! It is a book about life, and how we live this life that we have been given. And since God created all life, it's also about Him.

Let's remind ourselves of the first fundamental belief from Chapter 3:

> *First and foremost – we must wholeheartedly believe that God does exist, that God is the creator of all things, and that God does have complete control over all things. Any refusal to accept this belief only further validates the truth of the next two beliefs, and the fact that each of us is held in bondage by Satan, some much longer than others.*

Therefore, God is naturally a part of everything. Any discussion of life, or anything that exists, by simple deduction should also include God, who created all things.

One of the biggest issues that we carry in modern times, for many different reasons, is that we attempt to do life without God. God is still there and continues to carry out His plans, regardless of whether we choose to be a part of those plans or not. It is God's world, not ours – His plans, His will, and His ways will come to realization no matter what we may choose to follow or believe.

Some may wonder why it seems like God isn't present in their lives, while others may even say that they've never seen any sign or evidence of Him. The simple answer to this lies in the choices that we make. In previous chapters we discussed what *free will* is, and the reason why God gave us this *free will*. God desires us to choose Him. When we choose not to pursue God and instead chase after and worship other things, we are essentially telling God that we don't want or need Him in our lives. Again, God will always give us what our hearts truly want and desire. We are the ones who have made the choice to live a life without Him, so don't go pointing the finger at God when you aren't seeing any signs or evidence that He actually exists.

The truth of the matter is, as we have also discussed, that our separation from God began many years ago in our lives. And as times goes on, we continue to grow further and further away from God, making it next to impossible for many of us to see that God does exist and that He is still there, right where He has always been.

If we truly desire God in our life and want to see the signs and evidence of God in our life – We can be certain that He will be there. The more that we seek Him out and desire Him, the more clear and evident He will become!

However, with that being said, this is not a book about religion. That may seem a bit puzzling, so, without trying to complicate matters too much, let me explain.

The world that we live in, which as a reminder is run by Satan, created religion. Religion was created by man, for man, and has been altered and modified by man countless times, most always in an attempt to please or satisfy his (or societies) current desires. The world has also taught us to accept religion as being something that is holy and spiritual.

According to Google, there were over 4,200 different religions through-out our world, and that was back in 2006. Twenty years later that number has now skyrocketed to over 10,000. Each one of them having different beliefs, views, or an understanding of what they believe to be true. And every one of them believing that their religion is the only true religion.

How can it be possible that there are 4,200 or even 10,000 correct view-points of what is supposed to be the same thing? The simple truth - It is not possible, in any way. The distortion of man's religious beliefs is a conversation for another day, and one which would fill the pages of many books. Simply put, however, our modern-day religions are the result of mankind's personal agenda in pursuit of his own perceptions and desires and were created through the use of mans flawed and limited perspective and understanding.

What we must come to understand is that God and Jesus are not religious. They are spiritual. In the book of Matthew, the entire 23rd chapter consists of Jesus rebuking the Pharisees, teachers of religious law, for the way that they understood religion. God and Jesus are not religious. To grow close to God, and Jesus, requires us to be spiritual, not religious.

We Are All Religious

What exactly is religion? The Merriam-Webster dictionary defines reli-gion as:

1a : the service and worship of God or the supernatural

b: belief in or devotion to religious faith or observance

c: the state of a person in the religious life

2 a: set or system of religious attitudes, beliefs, and ways of doing things

3 a: cause, principle, or system of beliefs held with faith and strong feeling[1]

Therefore, according to the 2nd and 3rd definitions of religion, we are all religious. Even those of us who insist that we are non-religious, an atheist, or agnostic.

We all have passions and desires that we chase after in our lives. The things that we eventually end up devoting the majority of our attentions and time to. Hobbies, sports, interests, a career, and even other people. These other things become our religion. They become what we believe in, what we have strong feelings for, and what we build our lives around. These other things then become the first definition of religion as listed above – they become what we serve and worship, and they become our God.

All of us are disciples as well. The word disciple appears 261 times in the New Testament of the Bible, mostly in the Gospels of Matthew, Mark, Luke, and John, as well as in the book of Acts. The English word "disciple" derives from the Late Latin word for "pupil". A disciple is a follower or a devotee of a teaching. Through its application in the books of the Bible, we have come to understand a disciple as one who followed and learned from Jesus.

In our technologically advanced day and age, most of us are disciples of the Internet. This is what we follow and the source for all the information that we seek and acquire. If we have a question – we ask the Internet. If we need to know how to do something – we ask the Internet. If we need information – we ask the Internet. If we seek pleasure and amusement – we ask the Internet.

We have become a society of people that instinctively turn to a computer for all of our needs and instruction – and then blindly follow what we are led to believe as being true and accurate.

So, in one sense or another, every one of us has a religion and every one of us is a disciple of something or someone.

Let that last sentence soak in for a bit.

What is your religion?

What or who are you a disciple of?

Spiritual Religion

As we have just learned, neither God nor Jesus is religious. They are spiritual. Religion has always been created by man. There are just about as many assumptions or theories for the creation of religion as there are religions themselves. From that of social cohesion to bring growing societies and groups of people into agreement and order, man's attempt at explaining the world and life itself, or an attempt at explaining the inexplicable. The list goes on and on.

Our religions, just like the reasonings we create to validate their existence, have all become misrepresented over time through the use of our flawed and distorted perspective. Referring to the Holy Bible, the Quran, the Vedas, and the Tripitaka – the books used by the four main religions in our world today and accounting for over 77% of the global population, mankind has strayed greatly off course from their original intent and purpose which has now left modern-day society with a perception of religion that is far from appealing. The Holy Bible and the Quran, along with their religious leaders entrusted to convey an accurate message, have provided us an image of a God that is weak and careless.

It is of no great surprise that many people nowadays are leaving our churches and places of worship in search of something more fulfilling and promising. However, we must remember that our religious organizations are set up and run by man as well. They are not exempt from the attacks of Satan, and they too have been duped and deceived just as we have.

Just as unfortunate is the fact that the vast majority of our churches and places of worship are packed full of religious posers. Oh yes, my friends, the poser is very much alive and active in our religious institutions as well. People attempting to present the image of being religious, but then quickly reverting right back to their worldly life before they even make it out of the parking lot.

They have no relationship with God or Jesus, and any religious motive that they may have is solely for improving their own image. Again, my intentions are not to cast shame upon others. I actually know this poser persona very well as it is who I was for many, many years. It is a sad fact that every religious institution in the world has an excess of posers just like I was.

In no way do I intend to discredit or minimize the importance of our churches or places of worship. Worship and community are essential elements of every religion, and they should play a vital role in our existence as well. What we must wholeheartedly understand though, is that these places are not what our religion is based upon, and they should not be the completeness of our religious experience. They are an addition or an extension to our religion. Religion itself is not a bad thing and should not be shied away from. The harm comes from mankind through the distortion and misrepresentation of our religious beliefs, texts, and messages, along with the image and character of God and Jesus. Our religion should be solely based upon our intimate relationship with God, through His son Jesus Christ.

With an accurate perspective, we should then be able to see that the church is not God. Therefore, when we see or experience something that we may find offensive or uncomfortable in our church environment, we can rightly understand its origin, and that it is not coming from God and does not reflect the true character of God or what God should mean to us.

We simply cannot make sense of God based on the world that we live in.

"As obedient children, do not conform to the evil desires you had when you lived in ignorance. But just as he who called you is holy, so be holy in all you do; for it is written: "Be holy, because I am holy." 1 Peter 1:14-16

Chapter 11

Desire

We came across this word several times in the previous chapters. Desire – what exactly is it and what does it truly mean? We hear this word almost every day and commonly associate it with something that offers us pleasure or joy. The word *'desire'* can be used as both a noun and a verb.

The Merriam-Webster dictionary defines *desire* as:

- *conscious impulse toward something that promises enjoyment or satisfaction in its attainment* (noun)

- *to long or hope for: exhibit or feel desire for* (verb)[1]

Wikipedia has a much more detailed explanation of the word:

Desire is a state of mind that is expressed by terms like "wanting", "wishing", "longing" or "craving".

Desires are closely related to (the individual): they motivate the (individual) to realize them. For this to be possible, a desire has to be combined with a belief about which action would realize it. Desires present their objects in a favorable light, as something that appears to be good. Their fulfillment is normally experienced as pleasurable in contrast to the negative experience of failing to do so.

Besides causing actions and pleasures, desires also have various effects on the mental life. One of these effects is to frequently move the subject's attention to the object of desire, specifically to its positive features. Another effect of special interest to psychology is the tendency of desires to promote reward-based learning, for example, in the form of operant conditioning.

It is one important feature of desires that their fulfillment is pleasurable. In religion and philosophy, a distinction is sometimes made between higher and lower desires. Higher desires are commonly associated with spiritual or religious goals in contrast to lower desires, sometimes termed passions, which are concerned with bodily or sensory pleasures.

A desire for God is explicitly encouraged in various doctrines. Existentialists sometimes distinguish between authentic and inauthentic desires. Authentic desires express what the agent truly wants from deep within. An agent wants something inauthentically, on the other hand, if the agent is not fully identified with this desire, despite having it.

Within Christianity, desire is seen as something that can either lead a person towards God or away from him. Desire is not considered to be a bad thing in and of itself; rather, it is a powerful force within the human that, once submitted to the Lordship of Christ, can become a tool for good, for advancement, and for abundant living.[2]

The word desire comes from the Latin root words *De* and *Sire*, which literally means 'Of the Father'. However, just as we do with most everything in life, we have modified the meaning of the word desire multiple times over the years, as well as its origin and intention, only to suit our social needs and make something appear to be more acceptable.

Societies and cultures in general have always had the propensity of neglecting any endeavor to correct the flaws which may exist within oneself. Instead, we go to great lengths to alter the meaning and perception of any said flaw so that the flaw itself may be found as tolerable and the individual does not have to endure the painful process of change.

In an internet search on the history of the word desire, I came across a rather shocking article on the Merriam-Webster dictionary website. The short, one-page write up is titled *Desire and Consider: A History*.[3] While the author of the commentary is not mentioned, the article goes on to state: *"But etymology as a science is very much alive, and there is a newer theory" (for the evolution of the words). "According to this theory, consīderāre would originally have meant something like "to focus on the goal," and dēsīderāre something like "to miss the mark"." "But consider and desire may have at their etymological cores something more mundane than the heavens, something more suited for a quarterly update than a face upturned in wonder at the night sky. We are, of course, blameless. The fault is in the words themselves, not the stars or the dictionary."*[3]

Are you kidding me? The fault is in the words themselves? Quite an absolving conclusion to the article – which is basically the writer's way of saying *"We can come up with an absolute hog-wash opinion for the meaning of a word, but don't blame us, it is the fault of the word that it doesn't make sense."*

Perfect validation to my point – we change the meaning, and even the origin of the words, when we find that those words hold us to a higher standard. We dumb down the words and their meaning to make them fit into our lifestyles, instead of putting forth any effort to improve our lifestyles with the facts and truth.

Of The Father

With an understanding of the true and original meaning of the word desire, we can clearly derive that desire must come from the Father. It is also clear that throughout our entire existence there has been only two figures in any of our lives that have held the title of Father. Most of us commonly refer to our biological father as father. Those of us who did not know our biological father may have used this label in describing a man that assumed that role in our lives, through our mother remarrying or another man seeing a need and then stepping in to assume the responsibility.

The only other being that we have characterized as a father has been God, our Creator. God is our true Father and as our Father He has always had the intention of providing for our every need.

Therefore, if desire is 'of the father', it would have to be of or coming from one of the two father figures mentioned above. Now your family life may have been different than mine, but my biological father never instilled any desire in me. Sure, he showed me what it was to seek things, chase things, and want things. But all of these things were worldly desires and pleasures, which like many of us, I became very focused on obtaining.

Over my years I began to recognize that something inside of me was missing, that I had an emptiness or a thirst that I just could not quench. I'm sure that most all of you have had this same feeling at one time or another. Maybe what I desired was the wrong thing? After all, the desires that I had chased in the past had been far from successful at filling this void. Maybe I just needed to change my desires? Of course! I was sure that was it. My desires just needed to become more sophisticated and polished. What I needed was to stop thinking with the poverty mentality that I was raised in and start desiring the finer things in life. I needed to start thinking like the upper-class people, who were happy and content all the time. They surely had life figured out!

If you have spent any amount of time in this world, you too are very much aware of how this series of events plays out. And you too are very much aware of the emptiness which still exists within you, regardless of how sophisticated we may make our desires. It does not matter what we chase and desire in this world, for it will never satisfy the true desire that we have within us.

That desire that we have within us was given to us by God when He created us (of the father). That desire can only be satisfied and fulfilled by one thing – Joy!

Well gee, that's simple! Joy! All I need is joy to fill my barren soul and make my life complete? Yes...... and No! You see, when we think of joy, we think of the fun worldly things that bring us pleasure. A family vacation, a pleasure cruise around the Mediterranean, a sport or activity that we like to partake in, or for some, just reading a good book like this one. For me, I enjoy golf, I enjoy riding my Harley on a long winding road, I enjoy the outdoors, and I enjoy building things. But most of all, I enjoy my wife and kids, and now our grandkids.

But just as we have done with the word desire, we have also taken the word joy and dumbed it down to a meaning and understanding that will easily fit into our lives.

C.S. Lewis once said: *"Joy is never within our power and pleasure often is."*[4]

There are a billion things that can steal our joy, but only one source from which we can receive it.[5]

This joy that we desire comes from God alone. It is not something that we can produce on our own, nor something that we can find through any other individual or source. God created us with desire, so that in this desire we may choose to seek Him for this joy which then fulfills our lives.

Sound a bit far-fetched? Stop and look back on your life for a moment. How many times has that something which you thought would surely provide you happiness failed to be all that it was cracked up to be? How many times have you had your heart broken? How any times have your friends let you down or abandoned you? And why is it that no matter how many times, or how often, we take that extraordinary vacation or check that next item off our bucket list, we always come back feeling no better than we did when we left.

It never fails. We continually look for someone or something to fill us with this joy in hopes that it will make us complete. However, the end result is always the same. We always end up disappointed, and many times are left feeling like there must be something wrong with us because we can't find it no matter how hard we may try. The truth of the matter is that there is nothing wrong with us, as a person. The problem is not what we are looking for, but where we are looking.

Once again, our flawed and distorted perspective has steered us in the wrong direction, while leading us to believe that we will eventually find what we desperately search for in the world that we live in. In our search to create this joy on our own, we use that God given desire in an attempt at filling our emptiness with worldly pleasures. Meanwhile, that flawed perspective of our desire, which has been distorted by Satan, leads us further and further away from God, who is the only source of joy, and the true fulfillment of that desire that we have.

Yet another example of Satan's tactics – distortion and confusion. By simply confusing our understanding of the true meaning of joy and desire, Satan is able to get us to chase after our own pleasures instead of chasing after God. And from that point, Satan doesn't have to do anything. With the inaccurate information that we now have added to the database in our subconscious mind, we pretty much build our lives around these new beliefs and end up running down a road which takes us further and further away from God.

These two tactics are what primarily keeps the poser living a counterfeit life. Everything being distorted to keep us from knowing the truth, and constant confusion about who we are, what we perceive others to think about us, and where we perceive our value to come from.

Our desire was given to us by God with one main purpose - to seek out the joy which only God can provide us. With that said – we need to learn to thoroughly appreciate the relationship between God, Joy, and the world that we live in to be able to fully grasp the difference between joy and pleasure.

Pleasures are man-made, and can be created, initiated, and experienced by mankind within his/her own worldly powers and abilities. A simple example from my life would be – Golf. I love to golf. I get great pleasure from a round of golf, especially when I play well. I can go out and play a round of golf whenever I so choose to. And while God does control many of the factors that go into that round of golf, I do not need God to make that round of golf happen for me. I can pretty much golf when I want, where I want, and with whom I want to. That round of golf, no matter how great it may be, is a pleasure. You could even go as far as saying that it is enjoyable, however, it is not joy unless God decides to make it so and I decide to make God a part of that round.

Joy comes from God, and God alone. We cannot create joy on our own. We can only find it and obtain it through a deep and intimate relationship with God. Being God's children, He wants to lavish us with this joy all the time, just as any parent does with their children. However, just like any other parent, God is not going to fill our lives with joy if we choose not to acknowledge Him as our Father. He also will not fill our lives with joy if we continue to live the self-life, seeking our own pleasures and desires. We must fully submit our lives to God and choose to live in His will and His desires in order to partake in this joy.

Let's go back to that round of golf that I chose to partake in for pleasure. Prior to my great awakening, when God came into my life and made me aware of the truths and realities of our existence, I would go play golf all the time. It was what I desired and what I wanted to do. It was another day, another round of golf, with most of them being insignificant and unfulfilling. Sure, many of them were fun. Sure, I played some really great rounds and shot some really low scores. And yes, I had some memorable times with friends and family members as well. But not one of those rounds fulfilled me. Not one of those rounds made me complete. The one thing that I do remember from all of those rounds was that after every round I was always wanting to play again. Even after the bad rounds. What I came to realize was that I was always trying to play more, and to play better, just hoping that it would give me that feeling of complete joy.

I've played golf courses all over the country. Countless rounds year after year. I've set three course records, had seven holes-in-one, and shot countless rounds in the low sixties. I've played with Actors, Rock Stars, Politicians, Military Leaders, and thousands of other people that I don't even remember. None of it mattered. None of it was fulfilling. When the next day came around, I was back at it again, in search of that joy that I wasn't even aware I was looking for.

After I truly gave my life to God and His will and desires, the rounds of golf became different. I find now that I do not golf as often as I used to. Not because I no longer get pleasure from doing so, but because I am more focused on doing God's will and God has me doing many more important things. But as my loving Father, who cares for me greater than anyone ever could, every now and then He tells me that I need a break. God tells me that I need some joy in my life, so He makes it happen. God lays it all out. God tells me that I should go play with this person or that person, which I do. And when I go play that round of golf, it now becomes four to five hours of heartwarming treasures that God has enabled just for me. The beauties that I see during that round. The experiences that I encounter during that round. And the overall feeling of satisfaction and fullness after the round is over. It is as if God is right there with me, touching and influencing every aspect of my day, just to say I love you and your happiness means everything to Me.

I can play a round of golf anytime. But that round of golf is just something that I do until I come into full alignment with God and His will and desires. And once I do, that round of golf now becomes something mystical, something joyful.

Could it be that fulfilling our desires simply requires us to delight in the Lord? According to Psalm 37:4, it would appear so.

"Take delight in the Lord, and he will give you your heart's desires." Psalm 37:4
NLT

Could it be that the pleasures we chase are simply distractions to keep us from something deeper and more meaningful? According to John, it would appear so.

"For everything in the world—the lust of the flesh, the lust of the eyes, and the pride of life—comes not from the Father but from the world." 1 John 2:16

I think we can all agree that everyone has desires. The only questions that remain are:

What is it that we truly desire, and exactly where do we get these desires from?

What is it we pursue in the hope of filling that emptiness in our lives?

We should give ourselves the chance to see things from a different perspective. We need to think beyond the box in our minds, the one where we've already set predetermined boundaries.

We must allow ourselves to be open to the fact that much greater things exist in our reality and that they are fully attainable if we could only remove those constraints on our lives that were placed there by no one other than ourselves.

"Whom have I in heaven but you? And earth has nothing I desire besides you. My flesh and my heart may fail, but God is the strength of my heart and my portion forever." Psalm 73:25-26

Chapter 12

Who We Were Created to Be

A long time ago, in a garden far, far away...... God created man and placed him in this garden to live and rule forever. The place that we now know as the Garden of Eden was perfectly pure and genuine, being completely free from sin, corruption, and deception – if one can possibly envision such a place.

"So God created mankind in his own image, in the image of God he created them; male and female he created them." Genesis 1:27

Each and every one of us, whether we choose to believe in God or not, have been created in the image of God. An image is something or someone that strongly resembles another. We were created by God to closely reflect His essence, not just in our appearance but in many other profound ways as well.

The original intention for mankind, after being placed into the Garden, was that we would live in this perfect place forever. A world where God had already provided everything for us and would keep doing so as well. God had already created all of the plants and trees. God had already created all of the birds and animals. God had already created all of the land and sky. God had already created all of the fish and the seas. And God had given dominion over all of this to man.

"God blessed them and said to them, "Be fruitful and increase in number; fill the earth and subdue it. Rule over the fish in the sea and the birds in the sky and over every living creature that moves on the ground."" Genesis 1:28

Mankind had been placed into a perfect world, having every need provided for, and had been given authority to rule over all that God had created. Is it even possible for us living in today's day and age to imagine such a place? With the constant pressures and struggles that we face, being pushed and pulled in one direction or another, and the expectations that are forced upon us not only by others but more so by ourselves – it becomes extremely difficult for us to contemplate such a place as being a reality.

That's exactly who we were meant to be and how our lives were meant to be lived. Perfect, pure, and innocent. Free from all sin, shame, and guilt. Free from worry, stress, and pressure. Free from expectations and demands. All while being a strong resemblance of the One who created us. God has a word for all of this, and it is what we were created to be – Holy!

Well, I think it would be safe to say that all of us are aware of the disastrous attack which assaulted mankind after being placed into that garden. Satan and sin entered the world, and then mankind, as we fell victim to his lies and deception. This, however, is a key point in our history where so many of us today quickly mistake the true character and understanding of just who God is, and that the life changing effects of that sin were not His plan or desire.

Many of us have come to accept and believe that since God supposedly has control over all things, He must have allowed Satan to deceive mankind. Many of us also believe that as a result of this sin, in disobeying God, God is punishing mankind and continues to do so today by placing demands and expectations upon us that He knows we will never be able to meet. Others believe that while God may have created mankind, He has not been involved in our lives or this world since that creation, and everything that happens now simply happens by chance. Countless others believe there is no God, and that we are simply the result of evolution from a basic organic molecule that formed millions of years ago.

We find ourselves in a position now, thousands of years later, where the truth of the story, along with the character of God, have been so blurred over time that it is difficult for us to accept the authenticity of it. Much like a rumor which begins as one thing and then changes greatly by the time it reaches the tenth, twentieth, or hundredth person – so to has the true reality of our existence and the true character of our God. The story that we are told now-a-days, along with the image that we are presented with, are far from a true representation.

What we must actually understand and allow ourselves to hold as a core belief, is that God does not set us up for something just so that He can sit back and watch us fail. God doesn't just give up on us either. He never has and He never will. God is our Father, each and every one of us are His children, and as our Father He wants and desires the absolute best for us in every situation and in all of our lives. However, just as the case was when each of us were young children, what we think and perceive to be the best for us is most likely not. We are uninformed, uneducated, and inexperienced, to say the least. We like to think that we have an adequate knowledge of all things, but even the brightest of us is far from a clear understanding of the big picture.

We must also understand that God is not a dictator either, just waiting for us to screw up so that He may punish us in some way. God, our Father, wants only the very best for us. And because we are His children, He loves us more than we will ever comprehend. He gives us the freedom to make our own choices, just as we do with our own children. And just as we do with our own children when they disobey the rules or push the boundaries that we set for their protection, discipline is given for the purpose of strengthening and growing their character.

Another understanding that we should learn to grasp is that God is always true, faithful, and consistent. His character will never change or vary in any way. This, of course, is a good thing. It means that when God promises us something we can be assured that it will happen. It also means that since God is our loving, caring Father – He will always be there for us, as our loving and caring Father. It means that He has always wanted the best for us and that this fact will never change either.

However, it also means that God is faithful, true, and consistent to His own word as well. Therefore, as His children, when we disobey the rules or push the boundaries we can be assured that there will be discipline forthcoming. God does not allow, condone, or support disobedience or sin in any way. And He surely will not just ignore it either as if nothing ever happened.

This discipline is for our own growth and benefit and will transform us into a better person no matter how painful it may seem at the time. This discipline is done out of the love that God has for us, because He wants and desires the absolute best for us, and because He knows that our lives have so much more potential than what we are living today.

Yet again, it is our perspective and perception that has failed us. Our faulty perspective of who we are and who we were created to be has been diminished greatly due to an inaccurate perception of who God is, what His true character is, and what His true perspective of us is. The fault does not lie within God – it lies within each of us and our assumption that the view and knowledge that we possess is adequate.

Consequences

When I was in my teenage years, society utilized a practice which seemed for the most part to deter people from being irresponsible – Consequences. There were consequences for the actions one would take, good or bad. And since this practice had become acceptable by society as a whole, those consequences could and would come from any direction or individual. The consequences did not have to be doled out by some government official or law enforcement agency either. It was not uncommon at the time for these consequences to be applied by schoolteachers, other people's parents, friends, or even the average Joe whom you didn't even know. If a person stepped out of line and did something illegal, disrespectful, or harmful to another – they would almost always receive the consequences on the spot, by someone who was witness to the offense. Being an idiot was not tolerated, and no one else wanted to endure your BS.

Consequences are but one of God's laws and they apply to all things that exist. It is part of the character of God, which never changes or alters in any way. And since it is a never-changing part of who God is, it cannot be ignored or dismissed on occasion, such as one does when showing favoritism. However, because God is our loving father and is forever the same, these consequences can be just as much a blessing for our obedience as they are discipline for our disobedience.

While consequences may be delayed or put off for some time, they cannot be avoided. The law of consequences has been in force since the beginning of creation, and that fateful day in the garden when Eve took the apple from the tree. Adam and Eve were given a choice and chose to take the action of eating that apple from the one tree that had been forbidden. The consequences for their choices and actions were simply a law of creation which could not be avoided. It is not in God's character, or a benefit to us, to allow disobedience and sin to go unaddressed.

Adam and Eve had a choice on that fateful day – Remain obedient while trusting in God who had already provided them with everything that they could possibly ever want or need – or let some outsider deceive them into believing that there was a better way. They got greedy just as we always do in our choices. They wanted more than the everything that they had already been given. So, they crossed the boundary that had been set and fell victim to the schemes of Satan.

If you recall, God had given dominion over all of the earth to mankind when He created Adam. The world was his to control. Then Adam and Eve made that fateful choice and the consequences were inevitable. Discipline was administered by God on both mankind (Adam & Eve) and Satan. Adam and Eve were banished from the Garden of Eden and would now have to work the ground for all of their food. Women were forever given the pain during childbirth. And the dominion of the world was stripped from mankind and given to Satan for the time being. Mankind no longer had control over the world, it was now in the hands of Satan.

At this point some of you may be thinking – *What an evil God! How could He just give control of the world to Satan?* This line of thinking is also one of our tendencies when we ourselves take the inappropriate actions that we so often do. We blame God. How could He be so cruel and unfair? The truth of the matter is that God did not give the world to Satan, mankind did. God had given the world to mankind and had fully entrusted him with it. Mankind then made a costly choice, proving that he could not be trusted with such a thing.

God had created the world perfectly. God had created us, mankind, to be perfect and flawless as well. God had set everything up for us in this unblemished world so that we may live out an ideal, happy, fulfilling life. This is the way that

God wanted the world to be. This is the life that God wanted us to have and live. It was us, mankind, just as we commonly do today, that made the choice to walk away from God and a perfect life to pursue something else which we are deceived into believing will be better for us; but is only a lie given to us by the enemy who controls the world.

Good News

Pretty depressing story, isn't it? Unfortunately, that is our reality. That is the world that we live in today. A sin filled world controlled by Satan, with lies and deceptions at every turn. The prince of darkness continually trying to pull each and every one of us away from God and seeking to keep all others from ever knowing God. And doing so in such a delusive manner that we are unable to even recognize the attacks or the attacker himself. We blame ourselves, we blame others, and we even blame God for anything and everything that does not go our way – all while Satan sits back and relishes in the hostility, the chaos, and the division.

Yes, my friends, that is our world! The world which we live in and base our entire existence upon. However, the good news is that this does not have to be our world. The good news is that the truth is out there. I'm not talking about the so-called truth that the world wants us to accept and believe. I'm talking about the real truth. The truth that is undeniable and endures everything. And with a little help and guidance, we can find it!

"Then you will know the truth, and the truth will set you free." John 8:32

Jesus also tells us in John 14:6 – *"I am the way and the truth and the life. No one comes to the Father except through me."*

Jesus Christ is the truth. He is the way and the life. He is our answer to all things, and it is only through Him that the actual truth becomes evident to us. Without Christ, all other supposed truths that we hold are from the world, the world that is run and controlled by Satan, the father of lies. And we have come to accept these supposed truths through deception, when someone misled us into believing lies and falsehoods.

This reminds me of a billboard that I see on occasion when driving down the highway. It reads – *"Jesus will solve all of your problems"*. I've never been fond of this billboard. It has the intention of drawing non-believers to Christ, which is a good thing. My issue with this saying is that to truly believe that Jesus will solve all of your problems, you must first know the true character of Jesus. It leaves those who haven't experienced the true character of Jesus, such as the non-believer, to a quick response of – *"Ya, right!"*

So, when I claim that Jesus is our answer to all things, I am not implying that simply stepping up and accepting Christ as your Lord and Savior will make all of your problems go away. Jesus doesn't just swoop in on day one and give you a perfect life. It doesn't work that way, nor should it. It is a relationship, and one that we have to invest in. I can assure you, however, that when you do invest in that relationship, Jesus will be your answer to all things and will give you the perfect life.

Jesus is also the only way out of the poser life. As we discussed earlier, the poser is created out of a sense of shame. A faulty perception that we have of ourselves, most always brought on by our distorted view or understanding of an event or wound which we experienced. The shame is the lie that Satan feeds to us after that wound. Therefore, the life of the poser is entered into and built around a lie. (This would be a good time to remind everyone that we are all posers – and through simple deduction we would all therefore be living a lie.)

What if I told you that we would never be able to get back to that person who God initially created us to be? All of us were given the opportunity to build that life on our own. And what did we do? We chose to change that life into something completely different than what it was intended to be. In a sense, we told God that we did not like what He had created, so we created something better. So why then should we assume that we can just stroll back into that old life like nothing ever happened, and once again be in the good graces of God by doing so?

All of the questions in the preceding paragraph can be answered with one statement – Because He is God! The Almighty! The Great I Am! The Creator of all things.

And more importantly for us – He is God, our loving Father! The Father that loves and desires His children more than anything else. The Father that always wants the absolute best for His children and never gives up on them. The Father who is always waiting with open arms for us to return. The Father who has already forgiven us for every selfish choice that we had made in thinking we knew a better way.

The good news is that when we turn to Jesus and seek to know Him and be one with Him, we will not only be made aware of the truths, but we no longer have to live the lie that we have been living in our life as a poser. When we turn to Jesus and allow Him to be the main focal point in our lives, we are then set free from the bondage of the lies and deception which have held us captive in this false reality.

But wait...... The good news gets even better. Remember that perfect life that God had intended for mankind? Remember how God created us to be? That life is still there, waiting for us to claim it once again. When we live our lives in Christ and for Christ, we can actually go back and be the person that God created us to be. We can be ourselves – our true selves!

Okay...... I should probably expound on those comments as I can see that some of you may have gone a bit too far back in your recollection of 'creation'. It is true that we can go back and live the life that God had created us for. However, this does not mean that we are able to go ALL the way back to the perfect life that Adam and Eve were intended to live. Unfortunately, for now, sin is still a part of our world. That sin will only be done away with when Jesus returns and defeats Satan once and for all. Then, and only then, will all believers live a perfect life.

For now, we can go back to our beginning. That initial part of our lives when we were innocent and unaffected by the shame. The person we were prior to making that decision to become something other than who we were. That person which God had created and intended only you and me to be. We can let go and stop pretending. We can finally just be us, as God had intended, no matter who or what that may be.

We can finally have the freedom to just let go and stop pretending......... Let that thought soak in for a moment.

I understand that this can be challenging for many of us, as the person we once were feels like a distant memory at best. We don't know how to get back there, let alone where or who that person was. Our perception of the wounds which we have received, along with the pain and shame that accompanied them, have compelled us to distance ourselves as far as possible from who we once were, which inevitably drives us deeper into our poser persona and further away from that person we once were.

And while some of us may be able to recall tiny bits and pieces of that person, more than likely the images that we see will be blurry and fragmented at best. It won't be possible for us to clearly picture that person of our past from the distance that we have now placed ourselves from that person.

So how are we supposed to get back to the person that God created us to be when we have no memory of who that person was? How are we supposed to escape the bondage of the poser life when our true reality can only be seen in vague remnants? The mere thought of such an endeavor seems futile in every aspect.

The reality of our situation is that it is entirely possible for us to return. Back to a life where our confidence and freedom in who we are was never in question. Back to a life when all that we aspired to be was ourselves, not something else dictated by the pressures and influences of others. Back to a life of peace and easiness, without all of the fear and hatred. Back to a life where we lived the way that we wanted to, instead of a way that we think others want us to.

While it may not be easy, it is entirely possible, and well worth the trip. I spent most of my adult life deeply entrenched in the life of the poser. I was one of the lucky few who managed to find my way out and make it back. In the chapters ahead, I'll show you the way out—how you can break free from the poser life and find your way back too.

"Therefore, you shall love the Lord your God, and keep His charge, His statutes, His judgments, and His commandments always."
Deuteronomy 11:1 NKJV

Chapter 13

Reprogramming

Beliefs

Just as it was many years ago with Adam and Eve when our world began, we quickly lose sight of who we are, who we were created to be, and what truth and reality actually are. This, without question, is just one piece of Satan's grand scheme and always has been since that fateful day in the garden.

Think about that for a moment. If everything which exists in our world was the actual truth – not only would we stand firm in and be strongly convicted about the beliefs that we hold, but we would also be very confident in who we are as a person. And not in the closed-minded, dogmatic, and arrogant sense that we are so accustomed to nowadays, but willingly and freely open with no need to be cautious or guarded. There would be no question of right or wrong, good or bad. There would be no misleading or confusing information causing us to question every action that we take. And there would be no deceitful attempts at diminishing the person that we are.

Unfortunately, we do not live in such a world. The world that we live in has become every man or woman for themselves, both having one common goal – to just survive. The world that we live in has become so polluted with falsehoods and disinformation that they are now the expectation instead of the exception.

They have become the standard that we now anticipate from others in almost everything that we do. Rarely do we allow ourselves to trust anyone anymore, as we have been taken advantage of too many times and the pain from always being on the losing end has become more than we can bear.

No, my friends, the world that we live in is anything but the truths. Don't get me wrong – the truth does still exist. It is still out there waiting to be realized. This, however, is where our travails begin. The truth does not always make itself glaringly obvious with flashing neon signs and lit up arrows to point it out. We have to seek it, we have to find it, and most often we have to filter through all of the lies and deceptions that try to bury it to keep us from seeing it.

Therein lies the difficulty. The father of lies, Satan, along with many of his followers, have been doing their thing for so long that they have become pretty darn good at it. Most of the time the lies, falsehoods, and disinformation are so good that when taken at face value they appear to be the truth as well. It becomes very difficult if not almost impossible to discern them from what is actually true. For a great number of us, we frequently fall victim to the deceptions and accept these lies and falsehoods as the truth. And once we have accepted them as being true – we make them a part of our belief system. They now become who we are and what we stand for.

What we believe and accept as true determines who we are and what we become. When we accept these fabrications as the truth, they become a part of our core beliefs. Our core beliefs are our fundamental, deeply held convictions about ourselves, others, and the world that we live in. Our core beliefs influence our thoughts, behaviors and emotions. Our core beliefs essentially determine how we react, respond, and deal with everything. And once we have accepted these lies as being the truth, we are basically building a foundation for our own life, as well as who we see ourselves to be, based upon a set of lies and false information.

Proverbs 4:23 states: *"Above all else, guard your heart, for everything you do flows from it."*

Hmmmm? Is that a typo? The verse doesn't say anything about our minds or beliefs.

No, it is not a typo. And it actually does say a lot about our mind. You see – as the verse says, everything that we do flows from our hearts. Our hearts are in a sense who we are, and they direct everything that we do. It is where our passions and desires come from, and what causes us to move in one direction or another. The things that we hold near and dear in our hearts, were initially taken in and processed by our minds. And once the mind finds these things to be of worth and value, we move them to our hearts where they become fundamental to who we are. Therefore, what we allow into our mind – the articles and books that we read, the shows and movies that we watch, the gossip that we partake in, the environment that we submerse ourselves in – all of these things are making their way into our mind, whether it be consciously or subconsciously, knowingly or unknowingly.

Therefore, what we allow into our minds becomes part of who we are and what we believe. We must be over cautious about what we expose ourselves to, and what we allow ourselves to accept as being real and true.

What we allow ourselves to believe also creates our sense of self-worth. If we succumb to the falsehoods and disinformation of the world, we can be guaranteed that our sense of self-worth will never amount to much. That is where the world wants us to be. Remember, it is every man/woman for themselves, and others cannot get a leg up on us by lifting us up or encouraging us. They have to keep us down, and one way they do so is through these falsehoods and disinformation.

The poser has a very low sense of self-worth and belief. Sure, their new persona may appear to be cocky and confident, but this is all part of the charade. The poser began accepting and believing the lies and falsehoods many, many years ago. Heck, for the most part, those lies and falsehoods were what convinced the poser that their original self wasn't good enough to begin with. And remember, the poser does not possess a solid set of core beliefs as they are always changing and modifying to adapt to their current environment.

The lies, deceptions, falsehoods, and the disinformation are all the ways of the world and of Satan. God and Jesus want us to know the truths, however. They want us to know who we are and who we were created to be. They want us to know the true and full potential that we were created with and intended to live in. And they want us to fully realize it as well.

Factory Reset

As we have come to understand, most everything that we have taken in to our minds over the course of our lives has been faulty or corrupted information. Nothing that exists in our world is exempt from these toxic infiltrations either. In the computer industry, this is known as a cyber-attack. A cyber-attack refers to an action designed to target a computer or any element of a computerized information system to change, destroy, or steal data, as well as exploit or harm a network. These attacks come in many forms and are known by names such as DoS, DDoS, phishing, ransomware, hijacking, spoofing, and countless others.[1]

Just as is the case with computers, each one of us has been targeted for an attack with the intent to change, destroy, or steal data; as well as exploit or harm our network, or the life that we were created to live. The main target of these attacks is our mind, as once again, what we allow into our mind will eventually shape and determine who and what we become. If the enemy can change, destroy, or harm our way of thinking, he can essentially get us to reprogram our mind in such a way that it alters the course of our lives, ultimately derailing us from the life that we were created to live.

The sad but true part of this analogy is that for almost all of us this derailment has already occurred. The attacks came long ago, and unable to see the deception for what it was, we bought into the lies and disinformation and then altered the course of our lives by believing these falsehoods and accepting them as our new reality.

And just as is the case with the computers, if the attacks are not fought off during the initial onset, the infiltrator quickly takes over and is able to corrupt all of the data that the operating system (our minds) utilizes to perform the tasks that it was created for.

With us, and our human mind, we quickly lose sight of the truths as well as all of the other information we were created with which would enable us to achieve the purpose and intent for our lives. All of the data and information that we were created with has now been erased and replaced with lies and deceptions.

Those in the computer industry have become very much aware of these attacks. While the attackers are creating new ways to infiltrate computer systems all the time, those that make the computers, and their programs, are just as aggressively coming up with ways to counter and prevent those attacks. However, not all attacks can be fought off. There are many times when the attacker successfully corrupts the entire operating system of a computer – just as is the case with most of us who have been derailed. When this happens, there is only one option that remains to bring restoration to the system.

In the computer industry, they call it a *factory reset*. This is a 'last resort' option intended to remove all of the corrupted data from the operating system, and return the operating system to its original factory state, the way it was created to be. The reason that this method is used only as a last resort is that it completely wipes or erases ALL data from the operating system – good and bad.

This process not only removes the unwanted data that is harming the system but will also erase any and all other data that may have been input into the system since its creation. This process enables the computer, or its operating system, to be salvageable and put into use once again for the purpose that it was created for. However, this process is never easy as it also requires one to input all of the good data back into the system once again since it too was erased.

The good news for us as human beings is that we too can have a factory reset. We can purge all of that corrupted data from our mind and reset our operating system to its original factory intent. We too can have a fresh start and go back to being the person that we were created to be. But much like the computer system, our factory reset will not be easy.

We have to wipe everything and start over, which will be a challenging feat for many of us. Why do we have to wipe everything, you may ask? For one simple reason – our operating system is corrupted. Over the years, we have allowed ourselves to absorb countless lies and an endless amount of disinformation.

We have likely reached a point that we no longer know or have the ability to discern what is true. At one point or another we allowed ourselves to accept these lies and falsehoods as being true and real. Therefore, it is almost a certainty that we would be unable to differentiate between the good and the bad information that we currently possess.

We are not allowed to pick and choose what stays or what goes either. It all has to go! If we truly want change then we have to realize and accept the fact that we have been trying to do this on our own for many years now – and it is just not working!

We have to be willing to open up and accept the help and advice of others – preferably others who have been down the same road. And then we must humble ourselves into following the advice and footsteps of those who have made it out.

To successfully leave our life as a poser behind we must be wholeheartedly committed to wiping the slate clean and completely renewing our mind.

Not an easy task, but:
Nothing of good ever comes easy, and nothing easy is ever of any good.

> *"You cannot change character or behavior and leave beliefs intact."*[2]

"For we must all appear before the judgment seat of Christ, so that each of us may receive what is due us for the things done while in the body, whether good or bad."
2 Corinthians 5:10

Chapter 14

A New Beginning

I am going to assume that since you turned the page instead of closing the book, you are committed to change, and you no longer desire to live your life as a poser. Congratulations! This is Step #1 - the first step – which is often the hardest step to take.

To successfully make any change in our life we must wholeheartedly commit to that change as well as the process that enables it. We must be all-in, and fully willing to take the next step, no matter how difficult or uncomfortable that next step may be. We must also learn to trust the process while understanding that the process is only a means to reach our desired goal. It is of no significance that we completely understand the entire process at this point; we only need to trust that it will enable us to reach our desired goal.

And we must, at all costs, avoid trying to take control of the process along the way. That is our old self-life, the poser, fighting for its survival. It has to go, and it has to go now! This point is paramount in our change because, as posers, our lives are centered around control. As posers, we seek to control, or at least perceive that we have control, over all aspects of our life in order to protect ourselves from returning to that person which we abandoned many years ago, that person which we see as undesirable.

Erasure

As mentioned in our last chapter, everything has to go. Every little piece of information and knowledge that we have acquired, obtained, learned, and possess – in regard to how we live, react and respond to this life and the world that we live in. While I say that everything must go, do not take this statement as an absolute, having no exceptions or restrictions. Even in the false life of the poser there are many beliefs which we hold that are true and factual and well worth keeping. For example – Your mother, your father, your spouse, your kids, your significant other – they love you; that is true and real. The memories and experiences that we have shared with these people are true and real as well. As long as those memories and experiences are good and uplifting, keep 'em.

What we are seeking is the truth. If we can honestly validate that something is true and factual, then we will keep it. It's all of that other garbage that we have come to accept as the truth which we need to dispose of.

However, we should quickly recall the end portions of Chapter 13 when determining whether something is true and factual – *"We have likely reached a point that we no longer know or have the ability to discern what is true. At one point or another we allowed ourselves to accept these lies and falsehoods as being true and real. Therefore, it is almost a certainty that we would be unable to differentiate between the good and the bad information that we currently possess."*

The biggest issue that we have as the poser is with our perception. How we see and perceive things to be. As we have learned, this faulty perception causes us to interpret matters and events in a way that is contradictory to reality. We then take those inaccurate interpretations and make them our new beliefs, building our lives around them. It is the way in which we view and perceive things that needs to change the most.

We have also learned that the vast majority of what we do, think and say is simply an automatic response that comes from our subconscious mind. The information that we have established in our subconscious mind has been created by our view and perception of our past events and experiences and is now pretty much on autopilot, running the whole show without any intentional effort from us. This information is for the most part corrupted data. Its garbage, its junk. The vast majority of this junk is what we need to erase, and we need to do so while in the process of learning a new way to perceive matters.

This is where our first big challenge comes in. Our subconscious mind runs and acts on its own, without any effort or intentional thought from us. So how do we get it to stop working so that we can quit making the same stupid mistakes over and over again, while at the same time beginning to replace that inaccurate information with new truths. Well, it is not easy. Especially at first. But it can be done – and you can do it!

Do you remember when you were back in grade school? If your school was like mine, you would occasionally go on field trips. A field trip was when the entire class would leave the school and go somewhere else for an educational experience. Our class took field trips to a local forest, a state fair, and several other places that were around town. Every time that there was an upcoming field trip, each kid had to take home a 'permission slip' and have it signed by their parents. This 'permission slip' stated that it was okay for the school to take the child away from school grounds, essentially giving the school permission. Without that signed permission slip, the school had no authority over that child outside of the school grounds.

This 'permission slip' is exactly how we are going to shut off our subconscious mind and take control of every single little thing that we do, think and say for the near future. We cannot trust our subconscious mind at this point, and therefore, we must revoke any and all permissions that we have allowed it. From this point forward, until we have reprogrammed our mind with the truths, we must now stop and put forth a conscious effort and intentional thought into every choice, decision, and response that we make. We are no longer allowed an automatic response, which would come from our subconscious mind. We no longer have permission to 'free wheel' it through life as we have been.

Think of it this way – I have four children, three boys and one girl. They are all grown now and off to lives of their own. When they were younger, living in our home and under our supervision, both my wife and I intentionally set out to instill good morals and values within them, preparing them for the world and a life on their own. In doing so, each child was entrusted with a certain level of responsibility dependent upon their age and how well they had handled previous responsibilities they had been given. As each child would show that they were able to handle the responsibilities that had been given, they would be entrusted with greater responsibilities.

If you are a parent, you very well know that this is not a one-way street. It is not uncommon to find a child that is either not prepared for the responsibilities they have been given, or they simply choose to do things their own way, which oftentimes they feel is the better way. Either way, the responsibilities given to that child must be retracted and the process must revert to a lessor state. Any responsibilities and/or privileges given to that child are now taken away. That child no longer has permission to function at that previous level of trust. And, like me, if you have had rebellious teenage boys, there are times when that level of trust and permissions is completely taken away. When they can no longer be trusted by themselves, or in any choice or decision that they make. They must be supervised at all times as they have proven that they cannot be trusted.

This is the level of trust and permission that we must now give (or take away from) our subconscious mind – ZERO! It must be supervised at all times. We must carefully watch and scrutinize everything that it attempts to do and say, and we must be the ones who regulate what it sees, hears, and takes in.

Step 2

Next, I would like you to go back to Chapter 3 and re-read the first few pages (pages 24, 25 and 26). Go on – It should only take you a minute or two.

It is imperative that we possess these three fundamental beliefs for any true change to occur. However, it is not crucial that you fully understand the relationship of these three beliefs to the life of the poser right now, as they will become more evident as we go along.

Now that we hold those three beliefs – which are the truth – we are going to grasp on to them firmly and refer back to them every day until they become deeply rooted in our hearts. It would be a good idea to jot them down on an index card or sticky note so that you can refer back to them as needed.

These three beliefs will become our new foundation. Everything that we do, say, think, and believe going forward must align with these beliefs. If it does not, it is quickly discarded as we do not and cannot 'mix and match'. We cannot expect successful change if we are only partially invested in the process.

And since those three beliefs are now a part of our new person, we are not only going to live in those beliefs, but we are going to act according to those beliefs as well. If we truly believe something, it will become a part of who we are and what we do. One of my all-time favorite quotes is from the late Dallas Willard. Dallas states:

"Actions reveal beliefs 100% of the time."[1]

In simple terms – Every little thing that we do and say, shows a clear picture of what our true beliefs and desires are.

Take a look at your life for a moment. What do the things that you do and say reveal about what you believe and desire?

Our first act of living in these new beliefs is through our acknowledgment that God is the Creator of all things, that God is our loving Father and Provider, and that we alone cannot succeed in anything outside of the will of our Father. (It is the truth, I can assure you. That resistance you are feeling is the reluctance of your poser persona to acknowledge that someone else may be in control.)

Therefore, one of the most important things that we will do moving forward is to pray. We pray to God to offer up our praise and thanks for all that He has done for us and has planned for our future, and we pray to ask for His guidance and His will. Most importantly, we pray to remain in union with God and Christ. It is one way that we communicate with God, Jesus, and the Holy Spirit, which is vital and required in any relationship.

Many of you may not be comfortable praying at this point. This is perfectly normal. Just like you did at the beginning of this chapter – it just takes that first step. The first is always the hardest. From there it's all downhill. Don't feel like you have to be good at it either, that again is the view that the world wants us to see. Remove the pressures and perceptions that we have been forced to accept about prayer and religion and just be you. That is all that God wants – the true and real you! Not the poser, and not someone pretending like they know how it all works.

I remember when I first began to pray. Now there was a sight to see! Several months prior to that I had a divine experience with the presence of God, which led me to seek and desire Him like nothing else. I wanted to know more. I wanted to know the truths. I wanted to know what was real and who He really was. My problem was that I had no clue how to pray. I had no religious background, and these were things that were not a part of my life growing up. I didn't know what to do, how to do it, or where to begin. God was well aware of all this, and He wanted me just the way that I was. He just wanted me to come to Him. He could, and eventually would, teach me how to pray – after all, He did create everything.

My first prayers were a few moments of me basically bowing my head, closing my eyes and crying out to God. I didn't feel worthy enough to be praying to Him, and I surely didn't have the big words and fancy formats that we so commonly see today. I went on for a couple weeks in this manner, receiving no divine revelation of how God wanted me to pray. But every day, I would continue to show up and try. Then one day I heard His voice – He told me how to pray, or how He wanted me to pray.

What I heard from God on that day really opened my eyes about who He is and about His character. I'm hoping that it will reveal some things to you as well. God told me that when I prayed to Him, it was only about me and Him. It was not about the world. He did not want the things that I had seen or learned from the world. He wanted me, and that was it. He wanted my heart and my full openness and honesty. He just wanted me to be me, and He just wanted me to come to him for everything.

It was as if a huge weight had been lifted off my shoulders. I didn't have to try to be something other than the true me. I didn't have to pretend or fake it. I just had to be me – fully open and fully honest. Over the next few days, I came to realize that God saying this to me meant so much more. I now understood that The Creator and Ruler of all things, The Most High, The Mighty and All-Powerful God wanted me, desired me, and loved me just the way that I am and that me simply being me was more than good enough. It still overwhelms me to this day that All-Mighty God, the Creator of the Heavens and Earth, desires nothing more than for insignificant, little ole me to just come and spend time with Him.

My prayers have now evolved into something a bit more detailed and lengthier. I also no longer pray, or talk to God, just a few times a day. I am constantly in conversation with God, Jesus, and The Holy Spirit throughout my day. This, however, is not a result of my own desires but that of living in The Spirit. It is God that has impressed this upon me, and God that has drawn me near revealing His desires and will to me.

As we venture into anything, we should seek the Father's guidance and blessings. Therefore, since we are about to venture into a major change in our life, it would be fitting to act upon our new beliefs by turning to our Father in prayer and asking for His support and guidance.

Read the following prayer aloud, if possible, and then we will continue our transformation in the next chapter.

Father, Jesus, Holy Spirit – Thank you Lord for this day that you have given me. Thank you for removing the veil of darkness from my eyes and my life and allowing me to see your truths. Thank you, Lord, for loving me, desiring me, and choosing me. Thank you for calling my name before I was born.

I pray, Lord, that you would forgive me of my sins. Forgive me of my selfish desires and for not living the life that you created for me. Forgive me Father for turning from you and for believing the lies and deceptions of this world. I pray that you would continue to reveal to me your truths and your will and that you would direct me and guide me in all of my ways, according to your will.

Jesus – Thank you for the sacrifice that you made for my sins. Thank you for the new life that you have given me, and for freeing me from the bondage of sin and death. I choose to follow you Jesus, and to live in you and through you for all of my days. Come into me, heal me, cleanse me and renew me. Restore our union, Lord, and draw me close to you.

Holy Spirit – I grant you full and complete access to all of my mind, my heart, my soul, and my spirit. Restore me and renew me. Fill me with your true and perfect word. Allow the river of life to flow through me. Guard me and protect me from the darkness, the lies and deceptions, allowing only your true and faithful word to overcome me. Lead me and guide me in the ways and will of my Father, for His glory and honor alone.

I now renounce the self-life and choose to abide in you and follow you, Lord, in all that I am and do. Show me Lord, the person that you created me to be, and the gifts that you have created within me to glorify your name and your kingdom.

Amen

"Therefore, if anyone is in Christ, the new creation has come: The old has gone, the new is here!" 2 Corinthians 5:17

Chapter 15

The Change

After the first few steps in our journey of change, and our prayer, you may be optimistically feeling a bit less burdened. However, just as I was, you may also be slightly confused by this new feeling that is trying to overtake you. What you are experiencing is but a brief glimpse into what true freedom looks and feels like. And while you may not be exactly sure what this is, it more than likely has you craving more.

What you are experiencing is the power of God coming upon you and working in your life through His Holy Spirit. It's not by accident or mere coincidence that you happen to be reading this book, or that you have made it this far in the book. God is calling out to you. God is attempting to draw you near. The only question that remains is – will you answer, or will you just chalk the whole experience up to being something illogical or unreasonable and go right back to living life as you always do.

You see – God truly cares about each and every one of us and His primary desire is to make our lives greater than we could ever imagine. What we must understand, however, is that God is not going to just show up and do it all on His own. It has to involve us – we have to take the initiative. (That free will thing we discussed earlier)

It is a relationship, and any relationship takes two to make it work. God has been there the entire time just waiting to be involved in our lives. What He is waiting for is us to come to Him and say that we want Him in our lives. And once we do take that step, and continue to strengthen that relationship, God will work wonders in our lives that are unexplainable.

I am also aware that some may not be experiencing these feelings just yet. Don't worry. This is not unusual either. God wants to make sure that what we are doing, what we are saying, and what we are feeling is truly coming from our hearts. That we are truly in it for the long haul and are truly committed to Him and to change. It takes ongoing, constant effort and intention to build any relationship and to make that relationship the best that it can be. So, don't give up hope. Stay the course and remain in the process.

We didn't become the poser that we are overnight. It took us many, many years to stray as far as we have and become what we are today. Our transformation and return to that person we were created to be will not happen overnight either. That too will take many, many years. But with patience, persistence, and God's guidance, we will every day grow closer and closer to that perfect life that God intended for us to live.

Let's take a quick look back at the first steps of our change before we dive deeper into the process.

- Erasure – we have realized that every little piece of information and knowledge that we have acquired, obtained, learned, and possess – in regard to how we live, react and respond to this life and the world that we live in – must go!

- Three fundamental beliefs – the beginning of our new foundation starts with accepting and believing that:

1) God does exist and is the Creator and Controller of all things.
2) Satan does exist and he is active in our lives each and every day.

3) The Bible is the true word of God, it was inspired by God, and it has just as much relevance to our lives today as it did two thousand years ago.

- Our actions reveal what our beliefs are – the things that we do and say show our true character and what it is that we truly believe. Therefore, since we are erasing all of our old beliefs and replacing them with our three new fundamental beliefs, these three new fundamental beliefs define who we are and what we do and say going forward.

- We must live in our new beliefs – One of the most important things that we will do moving forward is to pray. Our prayer is the communication and union that is required in any relationship enabling it to thrive and flourish.

Step 3

Healing

Without question, the most important part of our change is in understanding the cause of the poser persona that we took on. We ventured into the life of a poser as the result of the wounds which were inflicted upon us by Satan in an attempt to keep us from becoming the person that God had created and intended for us to be. Satan does not want us to become aware of or realize the true potential that lies within each and every one of us.

If you recall, prior to his rebellion against God, Satan was one of the most powerful angels in Heaven. Before he was cast down from Heaven, Satan was considered to be one of the three most powerful angels, otherwise known as Archangels. To this day, Satan still possesses power, wisdom, knowledge, and abilities that we are unable to fully comprehend.

A significant understanding that we must also learn to embrace as one of our newly found truths is that of our free will. God gave each and every one of us free will, or the freedom of choice. We'll take a more in-depth look at the process of making choices later in this chapter. For now, we'll briefly touch on how that free will relates to Satan and our lives.

In a very simplistic way, think of it this way – You are one of the greatest things ever created. A prized and valued individual. Because you hold such value, you are wanted and desired by both sides, by God and Satan. They both promise you great and enticing advantages. At first glance, both offers appear quite appealing. You must make a choice – one or the other – there is no other option. However, the choice, the decision, the free will is all ours to make – to choose whichever option we would like.

> *"People are not in bondage because of past traumas; they are in bondage to the LIES they believed as a result of past traumas."*[1]

And, just as God will not come into your life and force you to love Him and follow Him, Satan cannot force you too either. The choice has to be made by you, by me, by each one of us. Unfortunately, as we will learn later in this chapter, many choices or decisions that we are faced with do not come with a 'warning label'. And when we made the choice to become something other than the person that we were created to be, in becoming a poser, we chose to walk away from God and to follow Satan and the ways of the world.

> *"It is the image of God reflected in you that so enrages hell, it is this at which the demons hurl their mightiest weapons."*[2]

To be able to fully return to the person who we were created to be and leave the poser life behind us, those wounds that have been inflicted upon us must be dealt with and healed. The healing of those wounds which we received from Satan can be healed in one way, and one way only. Through the life and blood of Jesus Christ.

Jesus was crucified, buried, and resurrected from the grave to conquer sin and death. The sacrifice of His life was the atonement for our sin. It was the cost that had to be paid to free us from the bondage of sin and the resulting death from that sin. Jesus is the only way to defeating sin, as well as the death and bondage that come along with it. And it is only through a life devoted to Christ that true freedom exists and can be obtained.

It is when we fully accept Jesus Christ as our Lord and Savior, and choose to follow Him, that our healing begins. The choice is fully ours, with our free will. If you have not already committed your life to Christ, now would be a great time to do so. In fact, it was through Him and for Him that you managed to get to page 160 in this book.

If you are ready to commit your life to the grace, healing, and forgiveness of Jesus Christ; I have added a small prayer below to help you get there. Say it out loud and say it from your heart.

Jesus – I ask you to come into my life. I ask you to heal me, redeem me, and make me new again. I accept you as my Lord and Savior and choose you over the self-life and the ways of this world. I choose to follow you, obey you, and seek you. Forgive me for all of my sins and cleanse me with the blood of your sacrifice. I renounce any and all agreements and covenants that I have made with Satan, with this world, with sin, and with the powers and forces of darkness. I surrender my life to you, as you gave your life for me. Fill me with the Holy Spirit and lead me and guide me in a way that honors and glorifies you and you alone. – Amen

Change

Like any road that we may venture down in life, it behooves us to not only know where we are going, but to know the route which we are taking in that process as well. We need a map, or guide, to help us in reaching a desired destination, goal, or outcome which we are not familiar with. This map, or guide, enables us to achieve our desired intention more quickly and efficiently, while keeping us focused on the change and not allowing us to stray too far from the process itself.

Is it possible to reach our destination without the map or guide? Well, yes, it is possible. This, in fact, is exactly how most people live their lives. Aimlessly dragging themselves through each and every day of life with no plan or intention. Just letting the whole world pass by as they simply go through the motions only trying to survive. And while it is possible but not likely, some of these people may too have dreams, goals, or aspirations – but they will spend their entire lives hopelessly trying to reach them as they have no map or guide showing them how to get there.

Once again, the flaw lies within our perception. And since our perception is flawed – We don't see things as they are, we see things as we are. So, when we try to reach a goal or destination that we have never been to before without a map or guide, we are essentially saying – *"I don't know where I am going, but I know exactly how to get there."*

> **We don't see things as they are, we see things as we are.**

"We now live in the outcome of a largely unconscious historical drift over many years. Moreover, it is human nature to resist deep inward change, for such change threatens our sense of personal identity." [3]

Step 4

Choices

"Everyone is a product of their heredity, environment, experience, and choices."[4]

The next step in our process of reconnecting with that person who we were truly created to be, and leaving our life as a poser, involves recognizing all of the choices that are presented to us every day, and then teaching ourselves to make better choices or decisions that are based solely on our new fundamental beliefs.

Sounds pretty simple, doesn't it? Learning to recognize all of the choices presented to us each and every day. I can see that your mind is already working to come up with a number that it can correlate with how many decisions you likely make in a day, making it possible to envision just how difficult that task may be.

So, what number did you come up with? How many choices/decisions do you think you make in an average day? Twenty? Fifty? One hundred? Well, if that were the case, learning to recognize all of these choices as they are happening would not be such an arduous task. In reality, no matter where we are in life, that number is significantly higher.

In a recent article on PsychologyToday.com, Psychologist Eva Krockow states: *"the average person makes an eye-popping 35,000 choices per day...... roughly 2,000 decisions per hour or one decision every two seconds."*[5]

While Krockow does agree that not all decisions may be important in the grander scheme of things, she further states: *"even if it's rare—small choices can have big consequences."*[5]

This step in our process may prove to be the most challenging as our ability (or inability) to recognize these choices when they confront us can be a confusing process as well, for several reasons.

First, we have assumedly erased everything that we know and once believed to be true. Hopefully, we have also revoked all authority that had been given to our subconscious mind, not allowing it to make those habitual decisions any longer. Therefore, we must now actually stop and give intentional thought and reasoning to every choice and decision that we are faced with.

Therein lies our first dilemma – How are we supposed to make the right choice or decision when we hold no beliefs or historical data to help us determine if that choice may be right or wrong? This process can be a challenge and somewhat painful at first, but trust me, it gets easier as we go along.

Second, how can we possibly teach ourselves to make better choices and decisions when we lack the knowledge and experience required to do so? Our life as a poser has clearly shown that our ability to make correct choices is flawed at best. So, how is it that we are supposed to make these new choices and decisions on our own – while having the confidence that we are doing so correctly?

Think of it this way – We are resetting our minds and the extent of our knowledge to that of when we were a child. Going back to a time when we were learning new things every day. Our mind, our knowledge, and our perception were basically a blank canvas. A canvas which would one day display the full, completed picture of our life. We have now been given a new blank canvas to create a better and more meaningful picture with.

The truth is that while we have erased our past thoughts and perceptions, we still have our new core beliefs as our foundation to aid us in making all of our new choices and decisions. That is where we start. Every choice, every decision from this point forward must be validated and confirmed to align with our new core beliefs. These three new core beliefs will lead us into making the right choice and correct decision in every matter and will allow us to build upon those beliefs as we live our lives intentionally for God and Jesus.

We must also refrain from making choices or decisions that would take us out of or threaten the process of change that we are committed to. We must stay the course, no matter the cost.

So, when we feel overwhelmed in a situation, or maybe unsure what the correct choice or decision may be – look at it with excitement. This is our opportunity to paint that brush stroke onto the canvas as we want it to be, not as the world wants it to be. It can also be reassuring to know that children, those with empty minds and blank canvases, learn at a remarkable rate. Much faster than we do as grown adults.

Enjoy the process while you are in this stage. You won't be there for long. But remember – every choice that we make has consequences to it, one way or the other. And every choice that we make puts one more brush stroke on to that canvas of our life. What is it that you want your canvas to show?

What we all must eventually understand, however, is that the decision-making process is never straightforward or routine. All of us are confronted with thousands of choices each and every day. Most are fairly simple and have no significant impact on our lives or who we are as a person. However, many of the choices and decisions that we are faced with have long lasting, life changing results that not only affect our lives, but the lives of others as well. These tougher choices don't always come with a 'warning label' either, making us aware in advance that the outcome of this decision will be costly.

"Every time you make a choice, you are turning the central part of you, the part that chooses, into something a little different from what was before...you are slowly turning this central thing either into a heavenly creature or a hellish creature...to be one kind of creature is heaven; that is joy and peace and knowledge and power. To be the other means madness, horror, idiocy, rage, impotence, and eternal loneliness. Each of us at each moment is progressing to one state or the other."[6]

Beliefs

As we have hopefully learned by now – A significant part of our choice/decision making process is tied directly to our core beliefs. What we consider to be absolute. The ideologies which we truly believe deep down to our core and are unwilling to waver on.

The beliefs and ideologies held by the poser are the root cause and reasoning of the poser life itself. At some point in our past, each and every one of us experienced something which we then perceived to be diametrically different than its true meaning or intention. We then took our misunderstanding of that experience and made it a part of our core beliefs, yet again, through our flawed perception.

You know the story by now – the longer our life and this process go on, the worse it gets. The more that we view matters through our increasingly distorted perception, the worse the perspective gets. And all things going forward in our lives will be greatly influenced by this flawed perception, including our core beliefs.

A major truth that we need to grab hold of is the second fundamental belief listed on the second page of Chapter 3: *we must accept and believe that Satan exists as well, and that Satan is actively involved in our everyday lives whether we may choose to acknowledge that fact or not.*

> *"Human love has little regard for truth. It makes the truth relative, since nothing, not even the truth, must come between it and the be-loved person. "*
> 7
>
> Dietrich Bonhoeffer - Life Together

Understanding this fundamental belief and making it a part of our daily life is essential in not only knowing and understanding who we are, but in knowing and understanding the world around us as well as why and how things relate to each other. Once we begin to view our life with this reality, enabling us to become more aware of the lies and deceptions that bombard us, it is much easier to see through these lies and the disinformation, not allowing them to become a part of our beliefs.

Satan is the father of lies. All lies, falsehoods, disinformation, confusion, and deceptions come from him with the sole intention of keeping us from knowing the truth. This divisive act has been playing out for thousands of years and has so systematically infiltrated our world that what we have now is an existence that has fully given in to these lies, accepting them as reality and the norm, while adapting to their perversions in an attempt to fit in and be accepted.

This is the world that we live in – each and every day! And many, if not all of us, make the choice to accept and believe these lies. It is the story that confronts us day in and day out, and the story that most all of us build our lives around.

But since you have made it this far in the book – you now know that this is not the truth. This is not reality. This is not what we should center our beliefs around. And much like the canvas that we are recreating through our choices, who and what we choose to believe is entirely up to us. It is our choice, our life, and our story. Our reality is made up of the stories that we tell ourselves, what we allow ourselves to believe. Just remember – the choices that we make, no matter how big or small, determine who we become.

The only way a person's thoughts can have control over them is if they believe those thoughts. As soon as the lies are exposed, the power of the devil is broken.

What story are you going to believe?

"Genuine beliefs are made obvious by what people do. We always live up to our beliefs - or down to them, as the case may be. Nothing else is possible. It is the nature of belief."[8]

Step 5

Confidence

The next step in our process of change involves dealing with our confidence, or lack thereof. Confidence at the individual level is a skill and trait that is greatly lacking in our world today. The poser has no confidence in who they are or what they may believe in. If they did, there would be no reason for change.

Confidence, as defined by the Cambridge dictionary, is *a feeling of having little doubt about yourself and your abilities, or a feeling of trust in someone or something.*[9]

Having confidence in who we are or what we may have the ability to do is indirectly derived from our beliefs. If we have a strong belief system, and stand firm in what we believe, we become very confident in who we are as a person and what we stand for based upon those beliefs. We then have a foundation on which to stand. Therein, however, lies the primary issue in the lack of individual confidence in our world today.

Most people nowadays don't have a belief system. Most people nowadays just latch on to a view or belief that is popular, trendy, or attractive. It is a sad thing to say, but most people are sheep. They just follow what everyone else is doing, saying, or believing – and are willing to build their lives around the beliefs and agendas of someone else, oftentimes without even knowing what that agenda may be or what those core beliefs are. And when that someone else is no longer significant, we simply move on and change our views and beliefs to the next thing that we latch on to.

We do not have any confidence in ourselves and who we are simply because we ourselves don't know who we are. We are always trying to be someone else or to live by someone else's views or beliefs, therefore, it is impossible to have confidence in ourselves when we change who we are and what we believe every fifteen minutes.

The poser excels at this process. The commanding trait of a poser requires them to change and adapt to their current environment in search of that affirmation, validation, and appreciation. Any beliefs or values which they may hold have all been borrowed from their current surroundings in an effort to fit in and be acceptable. For the poser, having a belief system of their own would be contrary to their existence.

It is not possible for us to have confidence in ourselves mainly because the beliefs and values that most of us carry are not of our own making. The vast majority of who we are and what we believe has been formulated by someone else through their beliefs and perspective. We are essentially allowing others to determine the narrative for our story, or our life. Basically, we willingly allow others to determine what our story, or narrative, will say and how it will read. And in doing so, we are allowing others to determine the path and outcome of our life.

It is our story. It is our life. It should be told and read in the way and manner that we decide, not others. We need to rewrite our narrative and do so based upon our own personal beliefs and convictions.

"We simply go along with the many 'musts' and 'ought's' that have been handed on to us, and we live with them as if they were authentic translations of the Gospel of our Lord."[10]

Rebuilding our confidence in who we are is not something that happens overnight either. It takes intention, effort, and a great deal of self-reflection and thought. And since our confidence is indirectly derived from our beliefs, rebuilding that confidence begins by establishing a firm foundation of beliefs that we have entrusted through our own efforts and understanding.

As we learn to live in and act upon these new beliefs, our confidence in who we are and what we stand for will increase proportionately at a rate in which we do so.

"I will give you a new heart and put a new spirit in you; I will remove from you your heart of stone and give you a heart of flesh." Ezekiel 36:26

Chapter 16

Our Way Back

As we continue down the path of change, which will eventually lead us back to that person we were created to be, we should find ourselves abandoning the self-life and our own selfish pursuits and desires, replacing them with God's will and desires. This endeavor, that of relinquishing control and placing others before ourselves, is where many of us struggle to remain fully committed. As we already know, the poser has established their life around control, or at least the perceived control that they have erroneously led themselves to believe they may have.

The posers need for control is driven by fear. It is a defense mechanism that we utilize to create a false sense of security due to the fears which we possess such as the unknown, a negative outcome, or failure. Basically, we are afraid of these things, for one reason or another, and what we foresee to be the ensuing result should we encounter them. We conceive that if we have control, we then have the ability to eliminate any possibility of having to face any such fears.

Our fears were formed out of our past wounds and the ways in which we perceived those wounds to affect us. We have created these fears in an attempt to protect ourselves from the pain and trauma that we associate with those wounds. But as we have learned, our perception of not only the initial attack or wound, but the way in which we perceived it to affect us, is flawed and inaccurate. Could it be that our fears are then inaccurate and unfounded as well? I would think very much so!

What we must learn to comprehend, however, is that at no point have we ever had control, as far as the big picture is concerned. Letting go of the fictitious control that we do have only frees us to venture into greater arenas than we can imagine. It is in our belief that we need this perceived control, as a result of our fears, that we are kept in the bondage of those wounds, which were intended to do exactly that.

What we must also learn to hold as one of our new beliefs is that we were not created with this spirit of fear. It is not a part of who we truly are or of what we were intended to be. That fear, along with many other faulty beliefs, was cast upon us by Satan and the kingdom of darkness.

The Apostle Paul confirms this truth for us in 2 Timothy 1:7: *"For God has not given us a spirit of fear and timidity, but of power, love, and self-discipline."* *(NLT)*

This process of abandoning the self-life is better known as our transformation, which is also a part of our sanctification. To be sanctified is to be made holy and set aside for God's purpose. Our transformation is the process in which we actually give up our self-life to be more Christ like. Our transformation is more of the day-to-day changes within us that lead to our ultimate sanctification, spiritual maturity, and our holiness.

While our sanctification begins once we accept Jesus Christ as our Savior, it is much more than a one-time change occurring only at our conversion. It is a lifelong process. We are sanctified, or set aside for God's purpose, once we accept Christ as our Lord and Savior. However, it is through the lifelong process of our transformation that we will eventually become holy and spiritually mature.

A key point that we must also understand is that our change, our transformation, is a process. While we are sanctified and set aside for God's purpose once we accept Christ as our Savior, this does not make us perfect in any way. We will still stumble and make mistakes along the way. We are going to 'screw up' from time to time. And from time to time, we may even feel like we've made no progress at all.

These transgressions are a normal part of the process and to be expected. As long as we don't allow ourselves to stray too far off track, and we remain focused on the process. After all, God is more than aware that we are not perfect, and He does not expect us to be. He came to us, offering us unconditional forgiveness and love, regardless of how messed up we were or how many times we still may stumble.

So, when things seem like they are not working, we need to remember and stay focused on the process. There will be good days and there will be bad days. But the good days will get much better and far outweigh the bad if we stay focused on the process and don't fall victim to the negative thoughts and self-talk when things get tough and don't seem to be going as expected.

Step 6

Service

The life of a poser revolves entirely around their own interests. For some it is doing whatever they must in order to obtain that love, respect, admiration, and validation from others. For others it may be isolation which provides that sense of security and protection. For all posers, however, it is about control. The wounds which they have received, along with how the ensuing pain was perceived, have caused them to build a life where they are in complete control, or at least perceive that they are.

The life of the poser is very self-centered and egocentric. Very little thought, if any, is ever given to the needs, opinions, or desires of others. It would be self-destructive and counterintuitive to the poser's existence to put others before themselves. Doing so would require exposing themselves to potential harm, rejection, pain and embarrassment.

As we turn away from our poser persona, and the self-centered life, we are willingly going to open ourselves up to other people. We are going to learn how to serve others and place their needs and concerns before ours. This is a must in our process of change, and this one step alone will provide benefits greater than we could ever contemplate beforehand. At a minimum, the act of serving others and placing others before ourselves opens the door for God to work in our lives. It is an act of faith on our part – faith that we do trust in God and His complete goodness. God's grace initiates our service – Our faith moves us to participate through that service.

Does it sound a bit intimidating? Remember, the first step is always the hardest. And let me assure you, this one step, this simple venture into the lives of others – can be the most rewarding and fulfilling thing that you may ever do. I know – worldly logic tells us this doesn't make sense. How can giving to others be rewarding and fulfilling to me? Well, what we as posers have failed to realize is that this too is one God's laws. It is the way things work in reality, and it is a law that cannot be undone or ever changed.

Unfortunately for us, as posers, we believed the lie that had been fed to us that if we wanted something we had to go get it ourselves. We believed the lie that we could never have enough. We believed the lie that it is every man/woman for themselves. And we certainly believed the lie that nobody was going to look out for us so we better look out for ourselves.

Whether or not the other people whom we choose to serve reward us or compensate us in any way for what we may offer, we will still be recognized and rewarded for putting others before ourselves. This is simply a part of God's eternal and divine laws. Therefore, the God who wrote those laws and controls all things will more than make sure that we are taken care of.

Now, our reward or compensation may not happen the very minute that we do serve others, but I can assure you it will happen. This too is another aspect of the character of God – His timing is perfect, all the time. Our reward or compensation will come exactly when we need it most. That's the way our loving Father is. Perfect timing, just when we need it, so all of our needs are met as well.

A defective viewpoint that we hold which this service to others will help us to correct is in where we look to receive the admiration, validation, and affirmation that we so desperately desire. Being admired for who we truly are, receiving validation for our self-worth and what we do, and obtaining the affirmation that we truly are worthy, wanted, and desired – is only sufficient and fulfilling when it is received from God. Receiving these things from anyone else will only leave us empty as they will never be genuine, fulfilling, or long-lasting.

We must look to God and Jesus Christ alone for our admiration, validation, and affirmation. It is for them that we should choose to do everything that we do. And it is only through them, the Creators of everything, that our self-worth and value are determined.

So, what exactly is 'serving others'? What does it mean to place another person's needs before ours? And how do we go about doing it?

The process of serving and caring for others before ourselves is not a complicated one. However, for us as a poser it will likely be very challenging. We have spent years fine tuning our thought process to protect ourselves and to ensure that we get what we desire. It has become second nature for us to think and respond in a manner which protects and best suits our interests. And for many of us posers, it has become just like breathing, we don't even have to think about it – it just happens.

The world that we live in doesn't help us with this matter either. We spend all day being pushed, shoved, and pulled in every direction while at the same time being screamed at, cussed at, and belittled by everyone else. Very rarely does anyone ever want to lift us up, support us, or encourage us. It is no wonder that we are all trying to grab just the tiniest bit of anything that we can, for ourselves.

However difficult life may be, once again, we must remember that everyone else is just like we once were – stuck in the bondage of Satan. Most are lost souls just as we were. That rude, obnoxious person who berates you every day is really no different than you or me. The ugliness that is attacking you is not who they truly are. The only difference is that you and I now know the truth, and that a better reality awaits us. Remember—we need to adjust our perspective on where all this crap is really coming from.

Furthermore, yet again, these others are not the ones who determine whether we are worthy, valuable, or loved.

The Needs of Others

Once we learn the ability to place the needs of others before our own, serving others becomes much more commonplace in our lives.

To place the needs of others before ours, once again, we need to change our perspective. Are we beginning to notice a common theme here? That's right – our perspective. How we view things. It has been set askew since the days of our initial wounds, feeding us faulty information, and leading us to nothing other than self-destruction.

Our current perspective, or our viewpoint and understanding of matters, is one where we honestly believe that everyone else is out to cause us harm in some form or fashion, and that no one truly cares about us or our well-being. Yes, I am aware that there will be those who adamantly disagree with these statements. But to some extent, I can assure you that even the most selfless of us has moments with others where there is a deep place within that cannot fully allow trust or reliance.

Our perspective needs to change from that of self-preservation and personal desire to one where we put our needs aside and seek to fulfill the needs and desires of someone else. This too is a monumental task in the world which we are a part of as everyone is different, having different needs, different desires, and a different perspective. I am sure that we have all heard the saying *"You can please some of the people all of the time, you can please all of the people some of the time, but you can't please all of the people all of the time"*.

But what if we could please all of the people, all of the time? I know, not a very realistic expectation in our world. It is highly unlikely if not downright impossible to please everyone all the time. Mainly because we are so different, in so many ways. Each one of us sees things differently, having a different perspective on all matters. Each one of us also has different and varying levels of expectations, or how and what we feel a desired result or outcome should be. And with these different views and expectations, even the greatest of efforts can disappoint others as they were seeing and expecting something other than what we perceived the outcome to be.

Maybe our issue doesn't lie within what we are doing or how we are doing it. Maybe our issue lies with who it is that we are trying to please. As posers we were always trying to please ourselves. A pretty simple task since we know ourselves and know what it is that we want and desire. It seems that what we have now learned is that it's highly unlikely that we would be able to please everyone else. So, if we are to turn away from putting ourselves first, and it is also not possible to please everyone else – Who can we please, or place before ourselves and our needs?

There is only one that we should be placing before ourselves and seeking to please in everything that we do. That one is Jesus Christ. And once we change our perspective to place Jesus and His desires before our own, the act of helping and serving others becomes very easy. We do it because it is what Jesus wants us to do. We do it because He asked us to. And we do it for Jesus because Jesus laid down His life for ours, so that we may be free from the bondage of sin and death. It is the least that we could do, and we do it for others regardless of who they are, where they come from, or what they may look like.

With Jesus in our hearts and on our minds, we freely offer help and assistance to anyone, in any way that we have the ability to give. We do it for Jesus, regardless of what we may or may not receive in return. We again change our perspective, not focusing on the person or persons that we are doing things for, but instead focusing on Jesus Christ and the fact that we are doing what we are doing to serve Him and to place His needs and desires before ours. The truth is that we have already been given the eternal gift of freedom and salvation – It is us who owe everything to Christ for all that he has already given.

Our service to others must sincerely come from our heart as well. It must be intentional and something that we truly desire to do out of our love for Christ. If it is not out of love and from our heart, then the act itself is no different than that of our previous life as a poser – phony and counterfeit.

Who is this Jesus?

If you have come this far in the book, I'm sure that you have come to understand that it is not only a guide to leaving the life of the poser behind, but also a so-called 'religious' book. Both God and Jesus Christ have been brought up numerous times, and the book also bases the foundation of our change on the belief in God and Jesus Christ.

It is more likely than not, that while the poser may know who God and Jesus are, they truly do not know God and Jesus. They do not have an intimate, personal relationship with them. If they did, they would have abandoned the self-life and the life of the poser many years ago.

It is also highly likely that while many of us may claim to know God and Jesus, the true person and character of both God and Jesus that we have been indoctrinated to accept and believe in modern times is inaccurate and does not truly represent who they are. For most of us, the God and Jesus that we know and claim to have a relationship with, is the person and character of God and Jesus that the world wants us to know.

Remember, we live in a sin fallen world. A world run and dictated by Satan, the father of lies and deception.

For us to be able to return to that person we were created to be, we must first know and understand the qualities and character of the One who created us. Unfortunately, with the limited space allowed, these details will be brief. However, they should be sufficient to give us at least a basic understanding of our Creator, as well as who we were created to be. It is also important to note that while we may not fully understand or be able to grasp some of the information below, as is the case with many of the attributes of God, that too is okay. We are not supposed too.

Let's start at the top, so to speak, and work our way down.

A term that some may not be familiar with is 'The Trinity'. The Trinity is the foundational belief that God exists in three persons. God the Father, God the Son, and God the Holy Spirit. Three individual persons, but all being one God. While the word Trinity is found nowhere in the Bible, there are multiple verses of scripture that support its existence.

All three are one, and God is essentially all three. All three have always and will always exist. God created all things and therefore was in existence before the creation of our world. Since all three are one, both Jesus and the Holy Spirit have been in existence before our creation as well.

God (The Father) is the Creator of all things. God has always existed and always will exist. God created each and every one of us, along with every spec of the universe that we live in. He hung the stars, the moon, and the sun. He created every finite detail of not only our lives, but the world which we live in. He created all of the wonders and beauties in our world. He created the oceans, the deserts, the waterfalls, tropical oases, mountains, valleys, sunrises and sunsets. He created the coastal redwood trees in California, some reaching almost four hundred feet high. He created the Giant Sequoias which are an astonishing thirty feet wide. He created the Painted Hills in Oregon and the Painted Desert in Arizona. The Grand Canyon in the United States, Mount Everest in the Himalayas, and the North and South Poles. Victoria Falls in Zimbabwe with the world's largest curtain of falling water, the Patagonia in Chile and Argentina, the geothermal wonder of the Blue Lagoon in Iceland which is always naturally heated between 98 and 102 degrees, and the travertine terraces of Pumukkale in Turkey. God created all of it. And these are just a few of the wonders which God created and which He created for you and me to enjoy and take pleasure in.

And when God finished creating our world, and all of the beautiful things within it, He had one more creation in mind. God had saved His best work for last. His final creation, His masterpiece, was to be made in His image, reflecting who He truly is and was. His final piece of work was to live out life fully experiencing all of His joy, love and happiness. His final piece of work was......... YOU!

Yes, that is correct! God created you (and me) as His masterpiece. His work of perfection. And He intended for us to live a complete life full of joy and happiness, living in the beautiful world which He had created just for us.

That is our Father, our Creator. You see – God fully knew that He would create us and He fully intended to save His best work for last. He also knew that as His best work, He loved us more than anything else He had created. He loved us so much that He created a perfect world overflowing with beauty and joy for us to live in.

Unfortunately for us, Satan came into the picture. This was not God's plan, and God never wanted us to fall victim to the lies and deceptions either. However, we did, and we then chose to chase after something other than the perfection that we had been given.

The good news for us is that our Father, God, is faithful, consistent, and true to who He is. He didn't give up on us just because we gave up on Him. His love for us never stopped. And ever since that fateful day in the Garden, God has been constantly pursuing us, seeking us, desiring us, and trying to get us back. Why, might you ask? Because we are His greatest creation and He loves us more than anything He ever made.

So why is it then that our lives are not full of this joy and happiness? As we discussed in previous chapters, this is the result of Satan coming into the picture. The sin, the lies, the deception, the falsehoods. All being used as a weapon to lure us away from God and Jesus. And unfortunately for us, we believe them and succumb to them, subsequently being led away from that perfect life that we were created for.

However, this is where Jesus comes in.

Jesus Christ (The Son) has and will always exist as well. Jesus was present with God in the beginning of all creation (Genesis chapter 1). At that time Jesus was not the Jesus that we are familiar with in a worldly aspect. Before being born of the Virgin Mary and coming into our world, Jesus would have been known as a 'Christophany'. The Jesus that most of us know and picture nowadays is the man that walked the earth among us. This would be Jesus Christ, the Son of God

The conception, life, death, and resurrection of Jesus Christ most always become the significant difference between most religions. While many religions today do believe in God, they do not believe that Jesus was the Son of God or part of the Trinity. Many of these religions believe that Jesus was just a man, being no different than any of the rest of us. Some believe that he was a prophet, but still only a man. With many of these religions, the Bible ends with the Old Testament. They believe that the New Testament, the life of Jesus Christ, and the Gospel of Christ was simply made up by mankind.

The truth of the matter is that the life of Jesus as stated in the New Testament, and His divine transformation into a man, was declared and planned by God from the beginning of time. The book of Genesis clearly shows God punishing Adam and Eve, along with Satan, for choosing to disobey God's instruction. God then foreshadows the rule of Jesus Christ in Genesis 3:15 telling Satan that he will be crushed.

There are countless other verses of scripture in the Old Testament which declare the arrival of a savior. In the book of Isaiah, which was written seven hundred years before the birth of Christ, the Prophet Isaiah delivers a powerful message from God:

6"For to us a child is born, to us a son is given, and the government will be on his shoulders. And he will be called Wonderful Counselor, Mighty God, Everlasting Father, Prince of Peace. 7 Of the greatness of his government and peace there will be no end. He will reign on David's throne and over his kingdom, establishing and upholding it with justice and righteousness from that time on and forever. The zeal of the Lord Almighty will accomplish this."

Isaiah 9:6-7

God is always holy and righteous, just as He had planned for us to be. In His perfection, God does not and will not tolerate sin. He cannot and will not allow sin to go unchecked either. There must be and always will be consequences for any sin. The consequence for sin is death, or permanent separation from God. God does not want this separation, which is the reason why He has pursued us, calling out to us, over and over again. God wants us to turn from our sin and return to the life of perfection that He created for us. God knew very well that once sin had entered our world, we would need a Savior to reclaim our holiness and righteousness and save us from eternal separation and damnation.

In the Old Testament times before Jesus Christ came, people would make a sacrifice offering to God to cleanse them of their sins. People would sacrifice an animal, and the blood from that sacrifice would become the atonement for their sins, allowing them to stay in God's will and favor. These sacrifices had to be made by a 'High Priest', which was the only person that could come to God and be in the presence of God.

God knew once again that this act was less than sufficient. God desired an ongoing relationship with His people. God desired to be in constant union with His people. Therefore, God had planned the ultimate sacrifice which would cleanse all people of their sins, allowing us to go directly to God, and to be one with God.

That sacrifice was in the crucifixion of Jesus Christ. Jesus lived in our world while leading a perfect, sinless life in every way. It is through the perfect blood of His sacrifice, the atonement for our sins; and defeating death through His resurrection that we are able to ask forgiveness for our sins and be cleansed of all unrighteousness. It is only through Jesus Christ that mankind is able to have a relationship with God, and able to return to that life that we were created to live.

And once we have accepted Jesus Christ as our Lord and Savior, not only are all of our sins forgiven (past, present, and future), but we are also set free from the bondage of that sin and Satan. The darkness and evil no longer have a hold on us. We are FREE!!! Free from the sin, free from the guilt, and free from the shame that Satan uses to keep us trapped in that bondage. In Christ, there is no shame. Sure, we will occasionally stumble (sin) from time to time. But this sin is no longer who we are. This sin is no longer what we desire.

Jesus makes it clear when He says:
[6]*"I am the way and the truth and the life. No one comes to the Father except through me. [7]If you really know me, you will know my Father as well. From now on, you do know him and have seen him."* John 14:6-7

If you want to make sense of your life, you must learn to make sense of Jesus.[1]

The Holy Spirit has and always will exist as well. The Holy Spirit is the Spirit of God. And as promised to us through Jesus Christ, the Holy Spirit dwells within each of us that have accepted Christ as our Lord and Savior.

"I will send you the Helper from the Father. The Helper is the Spirit of truth who comes from the Father. When he comes, he will tell about me." John15:26 ERV

Christianity is the only religion with a true and living God. It is also the only religion where our God is actively pursuing us and involved in our lives daily. So why is it then that so few of us know the true character and desires of our Father and Jesus Christ? Why is it then that so few of us actually have a close, personal, intimate relationship with God and Christ?

The simple answer is that we choose not to. We choose to take the easy way out, which is what our mind is always trying to do. This is part of our survival instinct as well – our mind looking for the simplest way to do things in an effort to conserve energy. So, instead of digging in deeper, asking the hard questions, addressing the difficult answers, and seeking the truth ourselves – we simply follow the crowd, or the world, and just buy into who they say God and Christ are.

The truth is that both God and Jesus have such a deep passion and desire for us and our lives that they want nothing more than to be a part of it every day. They want nothing more than to show us who they truly are and what we truly mean to them.

Our difficulty in understanding this love, desire, and passion lies within our own personal experiences. Just as we discussed earlier, on our own, we will never be able to comprehend anything greater than the experiences of our past. The love, passion, and desire that God and Christ have for us is greater than anything we can and will ever experience in this world. Therefore, on our own, it will never be something that we can make sense of or comprehend.

The only way for us to fully and accurately understand and know God and Jesus, and who they are, is to turn to them and open up to them. Once we do, they will show us and reveal to us who they truly are in ways which no one else can.

I find it rather interesting that while other religions believe in and worship other gods, they do so with the same goal of attaining a certain level of perfection or salvation. However, Christianity is the only religion where our salvation and perfection are not based upon OUR works, or what we must do to achieve them.

All other religions have steps, a process, or a path that you must follow to guarantee your success. The primary issue with this thinking is that it is not possible for one to know if their salvation has been secured except through one's own validation. They can never be truly sure.

With Christianity, we only have to accept Jesus Christ as our Lord and Savior – God does the rest. And that we can be assured of!

While these details accurately reflect God and Jesus Christ, it would not be possible for me to fully highlight their person or character in this one book. There are many good authors out there, a few of which I have listed below, who have written many great books that would be enjoyable and beneficial to read.

Recommended Authors:
John Eldredge – WildatHeart.org
Dallas Willard
Dr. Neil T. Anderson
Dr. Ed Murphy
C.S. Lewis

"From the world's perspective, there are many places you can go to find comfort. But there is only one place you will find a hand to catch your tears and a heart to listen to your every longing. True peace comes only from God."[2] Charles Stanley

Chapter 17

Chariga

(the exception - original Hebrew)

The six steps outlined in the previous chapters are only the beginning of our restoration. There are countless other actions that we can and will take along the way as we leave the life of the poser behind. A significant point that we must recognize is that our transformation, our renewal, does not and will not come about solely through our own actions or intentions. That mentality is what led us into our life as a poser to begin with. That mindset and way of thinking must be erased as well.

There is only one action that we alone can take which will lead us out of our poser persona, and back to the life which we were created to live. It is only through our desire to turn to and live for Jesus Christ, followed by our actions which clearly show this desire, that we will ever be truly changed. Once we give our lives over to Christ, submitting to Him and desiring to live our lives as He did, Jesus will do the rest. Jesus will then lead us down the path to our complete restoration; showing us, leading us to, and walking with us through the remaining steps.

This path will be distinguishably different for each and every one of us as we are all at varying stages in our lives. Each of us have distinct wounds and we have perceived those wounds in different ways as well. However, if we are keeping our focus on Christ and following His direction and guidance, we will reach our end goal.

The Long Game

Many of you by now are arriving at the understanding that this is not a 'quick fix' scheme. That thought may be somewhat depressing as we had hopes of a quick change-over to the better life. Once again, that is our old way of thinking. It is what we have been taught by the world that we live in. We want something quick and easy so we can move on to the next quick and easy thing should this not work.

If we are honest with ourselves – we can take a look back at our lives and see that the 'quick and easy' which we have always opted for has never provided us anything meaningful or substantial. However, our subconscious mind is already looking past what is right in front of us to see what may come next.

The 'quick and easy' has taught us not to give focus or intention to what we have at the present moment. It has taught us not to get to close. It has taught us not to get personal and intimate. And it has taught us that no other person or experience is worth serious investment.

Back to Step 2 – we have to erase all of these indoctrinated beliefs that we once held and then learn to live our lives as Jesus did and does. A realistic assessment of our past reveals that the 'quick and easy' does not work; but we keep searching for it anyways, regardless of the fact that the end result is always the same. It is time for something new. It is time for a change.

> *"The definition of insanity is doing the same thing over and over again but expecting different results."*[1]

Change

Change is often uncomfortable, as it should be. We have to put forth a conscious thought, focus, effort, and intention to make it happen. Our brain does not like change. The human brain is designed to make as many things habitual as possible, requiring very little thought or effort on our part. This too is part of our survival instinct. Our brain conserves our energy by simplifying as many processes as possible. The brain is also designed to take the easy way out, whenever possible. It is constantly looking for ways to simplify matters, form habits that can be repeated without any thought, and preserve our life by conserving energy.

When we have to actually put forth a conscious effort to do or learn something new, it seems very taxing and awkward. Many people state that they feel lost, confused, or out of place. Others find it hard to focus and therefore are unable to retain any of the new information. And the older we get the more difficult the process becomes.

I played golf professionally for a brief period back in my twenty's. Having your name on your golf bag, as well as the title of a Professional Golfer, automatically draws other golfers to you. Golfers always want to play with the better player. They want to see how the professional goes about his craft and works his way around the course. They want to see him hit the shots that they have only dreamed of hitting. And every one of them is hoping to open up the professional just enough so that the secret to golf spills out, changing their lives and game forever. They too want the 'quick and easy' fix.

Golf is much like life – there is no secret. There is no magic potion or pill that you can take to suddenly become something other than who you were just five minutes ago. Golf, and life, take many years of dedicated focus and intention to master. It takes hard work, intention, focus, and effort.

On occasion I would give lessons, or tips, to other golfers. More so out of a desire to give back to the game and for the simple joy that I would see when someone was quickly able to hit the ball in a manner which they never had before. And just as we are all different in our walks of life, no two lessons would be the same. Each lesson would vary depending on the individual's physical ability and desire.

Each lesson did always have one common factor though. At the end of each lesson, I would inform the student what they could expect to see as far as results, so they would quickly know when they may be steering of track, and how to fine tune those results. I would always end the lesson or teaching with one saying: *"Change is uncomfortable. If what you are trying to do does not feel uncomfortable or awkward, then you are not doing it correctly. If it is not uncomfortable, you are more than likely reverting to your old ways, and the change will never happen."*

One of the most important life lessons that I discovered from my limited career as a golf professional is that I did not have to be the best at everything that I did to succeed. I just had to be consistent. I had to show up every day, willing to put in the work, and determined to be the best that I could be with the talents and abilities that I had.

When I would play golf with amateurs I would frequently get asked: *"Doesn't it get boring hitting the ball down the middle of every fairway?"* and *"Doesn't it get boring making pars all of the time?"* My simple answer to the questions every single time was: *"It never gets boring looking down at your scorecard and seeing a number in the sixties at the end of the day!"*

Same game, same course, same objective – but two totally different perspectives. I knew that what appeared to others as boring and mundane golf shots would be the process that led me to my end goal, that of a good score. I also knew that I had to show up day after day to become consistent in hitting those shots on a regular basis. Therefore, I began to cherish those non-heroic shots as I knew it was just a part of the process which would lead me to the true joy, that of shooting low scores.

Like Christ

The vast majority of this book details the life of a poser. As we have come to learn, the poser is one who is living a life other than what was intended for them. We've also realized that, to some degree, we are all posers. All of us attempt to be something or someone other than our true person, even if only on occasion.

My hope for every reader is that through this book you may achieve an awareness of your poser persona and then fully realize that there is so much more to who you are and who you were created to be. The life that we live, the person that we are, and our true potential are gravely limited in our life as a poser. This limitation, of course, is with intention and reason. After all, it is Satan who led us into this life with his lies and deceptions. And it is Satan who continues to keep us entrenched in this life, ensuring that we are unable to see even the slightest glimpse of who we were made to be.

The title for this chapter is Chariga, which is a Hebrew word meaning *exception, or deviation.*[2] The primary goal of this book is to make others aware of the life that we are living as a poser, and to then show the way out of that life, while encouraging them to live their own life as it was intended and created to be.

With that goal in mind, as well as the preceding sixteen chapters, you may find it slightly hypocritical when I offer a chariga (exception, deviation). There is one way that we can leave the life of the poser behind while at the same time imitating or attempting to be like someone other than our true self.

In 1 Thessalonians 1:6, the Apostle Paul states: *"You became imitators of us and of the Lord..."*
Paul also states in 1 Corinthians 4:16: *"Therefore I urge you to imitate me."*

The model that we should follow, the one that we can and should be imitating, is that of our Lord and Savior Jesus Christ. We should be living our lives fully and completely just as Christ lived His life. And yes, this is how we were created to live our lives, and what we were created to be. Everything that we think, do, say, and act out should be done with the sole purpose and intention of doing so as Christ would have.

Paul also uses the word "us" in the 1 Thessalonians verse, implying that we should imitate a group of people, other than Christ. Paul is referring to the other Apostles, the Disciples, and church leadership in this verse. Paul uses this group as a model as he has spent much time with them and truly knows that they themselves are fully devoted followers of Christ who live their lives modeling the life of Christ as well.

Our lives should be fully devoted and centered around Jesus Christ with an increasing desire and intention to become more and more like Him, which will then reveal itself clearly in our character and our habits.

The Apostle Paul makes another perplexing statement in 1 Corinthians 9:19-22, when he says:
[19] "Though I am free and belong to no one, I have made myself a slave to everyone, to win as many as possible. [20] To the Jews I became like a Jew, to win the Jews. To those under the law I became like one under the law (though I myself am not under the law), so as to win those under the law. [21] To those not having the law I became like one not having the law (though I am not free from God's law but am under

Christ's law), so as to win those not having the law. [22] To the weak I became weak, to win the weak. I have become all things to all people so that by all possible means I might save some."

WHAT?? Are you kidding me?

This sounds to me like Paul is being a POSER! He is trying to fit in with whatever group he may be with at the time just as we described in earlier chapters. He is trying to gain the favor and attention of others around him for his own benefit and gain. But wait...... then we read verse 23:

[23] *"I do all this for the sake of the gospel, that I may share in its blessings."*

Paul was adapting to the others around him and to whatever the situation may be. But at no time did Paul lose sight of his focus on Christ and who he was in Christ. In fact, Paul knew to his core that what he was doing was actually what Jesus called us to do – to share the gospel with all people. It is also what Jesus had done Himself. This is exactly what Paul was doing. Paul was changing his outer image only so that he may be welcomed within a particular group. However, Paul never compromised or changed who he was or what he was created to be. Paul remained true to himself, his beliefs, his character, his values, and more importantly to God his Creator.

Hmmm. Thinking back, if you recall the conversation that I was discussing in the introduction of this book, this is precisely what my friend was doing. It was also the issue that I rebuked him for, citing that we should never change who we are to fit in with others. Could it be that my friend may have been correct, to some extent?

What Paul details in his message is the act of imitation, or reproducing an action, behavior, or attitude in hopes of achieving a similar outcome or result. The Poser does the same thing, in one form or another, yet with different reasons and intentions. Imitating someone else in a manner such as Paul describes should in no way be confused with that of a Poser for one simple reason. The imitation of Godly people, or Jesus Christ for that matter, produces a character within us that we were originally created to have. Doing so returns us to the person we were originally created to be. It helps us get back to the person we once were. Yes, we change who we are in doing so, but we change back to our true selves and not something other than the person we were created to be.

Personal note

If we go back to Chapter 14, the first step in our process was Erasure. We learned that we need to erase all of the lies and deceptions that we have come to accept as our reality and which we have allowed to define us as a person. We need to take out the trash!

However, in this process, we need to be a bit picky about what we get rid of. We are not just 'wiping it all away'. As we discussed, there are still many truths within each of us, and many things which we should hold on to. And even though we chose at one point to go down a different path, that of the self-life, we must not forget that it is God who created us. No matter how far we may have strayed from the person that we were originally created to be, no matter how dark or ugly we may have become, there are still many pieces of that perfect creation within us that we DO want to keep. We just need to learn how to use those pieces for what they were truly intended for.

A perfect example within me was one little belief that I had, which I held firmly too, and which became part of my core beliefs. Over the years I had always believed that this one trait was something that I had come to accept as a result of the self-life that I lived. In reality, it was something that I had been gifted with from God, and something that I still use proudly today, albeit for a much better purpose.

My walk into the life of the poser began largely in part due to my parents and their actions and choices. I did not feel loved, wanted, or desired. I did not have others in my life to support me or encourage me. And I certainly did not have others in my life to help me, teach me, lead me, or guide me. From a very young age, this quickly led me to believe that I was on my own and no matter how badly I may need the support or help of others, it would never be something that I could count on or expect.

With the mentality that I was on my own, I literally taught myself to remove one word from my vocabulary and from my every belief. That word is *CAN'T*.

No matter how difficult or demanding something may have been, I would never say or even think the words *"I can't do this"*. I did not have that option. It was me or nothing else. If I didn't do it, If I didn't make it happen, If I didn't find my way out of it, If I didn't solve the problem – Nobody else would either. Matters would only compound and get worse if I was unable to bring about resolution.

And as happens with all of our beliefs, that twisted and flawed perspective continued to metastasize into other parts of my life. I then began to think and believe that I could do anything that I set my mind too. I know this is something that many of us are told growing up, with our parents having the best intentions and hopes for us, but my belief was more than that. It was my true belief. It was who I was. It defined me.

For most of us, we are taught to believe this when growing up, but then quickly give in to any possibility of it being true as the world beats us down and bombards us with the understanding that we will never amount to anything. I, however, truly and firmly believed that I could do anything, given the proper training and practice.

My justification for this belief was simple – If somebody else could do IT, no matter how complicated IT may be, then why would I not be able to do IT? The simple fact is that IT can be done, so why would I not be able to do IT? Sure, I may have to make a lot of changes in my life to do IT. Sure, I may have to go through some intensive training to do IT. But if someone else has already proven that IT can be done, why would I not be able to do IT as well? I wasn't physically handicapped or limited in any way, and I was a smart person who learned and adapted very quickly.

Recent studies show that by the time the average person reaches eighteen years of age they hear the word NO 148,000 times. That number equates to roughly twenty-two times per day for every day of their life. Toddlers hear the word NO an astounding four hundred times per day. If you have children, this will likely come as no surprise. Hearing the word NO is essentially being told that you can't have or do something. We, as human beings, are being programmed from a very young age to accept and believe that we are limited in what we can have or do. And after hearing the word for so long, we accept that belief as our reality and who we are.

Research also suggests that people only need to hear a message roughly three to seven times for it to sink in and accept it as true. This research is closely tied to the 'illusory truth effect' which shows that simply repeating a statement, even a false one, increases the likelihood that people will believe it is true. Repetition creates 'cognitive ease', making familiar information feel more believable, regardless of its accuracy. Hearing something as few as two times can increase our belief, with six to twenty exposures often being needed for deep learning and acceptance.

The most important takeaway from this research is that while repetition is essential for learning and persuasion, it does not necessarily make a statement true. This, however, is how we live our lives in today's day and age. It is how we build our core beliefs. We believe that something must be true, it must be reality, it must be the way things are – simply because we have heard it multiple times from different sources.

The real truth is that no one gets to decide or determine who we are as a person, nor should they. Nor should we be conforming to what others see us as, or the limits that they have put upon our lives. The real truth is that God is the only one who gets a say in who we are and what we become.

2 Corinthians 5:17 says: *"Therefore, if anyone is in Christ, the new creation has come: The old has gone, the new is here!"*

Ephesians 2:10 says: *"For we are God's handiwork, created in Christ Jesus to do good works, which God prepared in advance for us to do."*

Ephesians 4:24 says: *"...and to put on the new self, created to be like God in true righteousness and holiness."*

And Jesus Himself tells us in John 15:5: *"I am the vine; you are the branches. If you remain in me and I in you, you will bear much fruit; apart from me you can do nothing."*

It is only in Christ and through Christ that our true identity is revealed, allowing us to reach our full potential. It is only in Christ and through Christ that we are truly able to remove the word CAN'T from our vocabulary. For in Christ, we CAN accomplish anything!

".... while evildoers and impostors will go from bad to worse, deceiving and being deceived." 2 Timothy 3:14

Chapter 18

Awakening

I've spent most of my life pretending to be someone or something other than the person that I was meant to be. Now that I have been awakened and am able to see what true reality is, it saddens me greatly to witness so many others who are completely oblivious to the fact that the self-life, that of the poser, is their only perception of our existence. It hurts to see so many people, especially those I care about, caught up in this delusion, including my own children.

What frustrates me even more is trying to explain this 'new reality' to those who are still stuck in the self-life. It's too far-fetched for them to believe. It doesn't seem plausible or probable in their understanding of how things work. With that said – I totally get it. I was there too. And I'm sure there were countless times when someone made the attempt to help me see behind the curtain as well.

Some of you may have caught on to the unintentional irony in this book along the way. I wrote this book with the hopes of helping others see that their lives were intended to be, and still can be, so much more than the so-called reality that we have all come to accept. The book highlights the fact that we are all posers; one who has taken on a persona other than our true selves. The remaining chapters detail how we can free ourselves from that life as a poser and get back to the person that we were created to be. The irony plays out as I suggest you imitate me and the steps which allowed me to break free from this life.

The Goal

True Godliness is a genuine reverence toward God that governs one's attitude toward every aspect of life. This should be our goal and what we reshape our lives to become as we eradicate our poser life. We were created by God, and made to honor, obey, and glorify God in all that we do. The act of being a poser, even at the most basic level, is blasphemy, an act of great disrespect. The act of being a poser is a personal choice to turn from the one who created us, essentially saying *"I've got a better way to do things".*

When we choose True Godliness as our goal and choose to honor and obey God in all that we do, the change in our life and our person will be evident at all times.

Proverbs 16:7 says: *"When your ways please the Lord, He causes your enemies to be at peace with you."*

As a man thinketh, so he does. – Proverbs 23:7

As your faith is, so it shall be. – Matthew 9:29

C.S. Lewis wrote the following almost seventy-five years ago:
"It is a serious thing to live in a society of possible gods and goddesses, to remember that the dullest and most uninteresting person you may talk to may one day be a creature which, if you saw it now, you would be strongly tempted to worship, or else a horror and corruption such as you now meet, if at all, only in a nightmare. All day long we are, in some degree, helping each other to one or other of these destinations (heaven or hell). It is in the light of these overwhelming possibilities, it

is with the awe and the circumspection proper to them, that we should conduct all our dealings with one another, all friendships, all loves, all play, all politics. There are no ordinary people. You have never talked to a mere mortal. Nations, cultures, arts, civilization—these are mortal, and their life is to ours as the life of a gnat. But it is immortals whom we joke with, work with, marry, snub, and exploit— immortal horrors or everlasting splendors."[1]

Reading back through the Lewis statement two or three times, contemplating each sentence as you go along, there are a couple key assertions about our lives and who we truly are that catch your attention.

First – *There are no ordinary people.* Even the dullest and most uninteresting person may one day be a creature which we would either be tempted to worship or be in complete fear of (either being completely holy and righteous or completely evil).

Second – *All day long we are, in some degree, helping each other to one or the other of these destinations (heaven or hell).* It is in the way we act, the way we respond, the things that we say and do. It is our character, our persona, the person who we truly are that leaves an indelible stamp on the lives of others, often times guiding or directing them in one direction or another. Once again, we have a choice. We can choose who we are, what we stand for, and what we believe in – fully knowing that whatever that choice may be, the correlating actions of that choice will either lead others to heaven or to hell.

It was our choices which led us into the life of the poser. The ways in which we chose and still choose to perceive matters. The lies and deceptions that we chose and still choose to believe as being true, accepting them as being our reality. The choices that we made, and still do make, allowing other people and things a higher priority and status in our lives than God.

Sadly, we choose to continue down this road of poor choices, even while everything around us is crumbling and falling apart. We refuse to acknowledge the fact that the path we have chosen just isn't working. We blame ourselves for the failures and lack of success. We blame ourselves for never having peace, joy, or love. We blame ourselves for not having the so-called 'good life'. It must be our fault. We just aren't trying hard enough. We just aren't giving it our best. If only we could muster up the energy to give it everything within us, and also have these countless other problems go away, we could surely make it work.

On and on we go, always trying to make it work. Thinking that we alone can solve this problem called life. The true reality of the situation is that the problem is much greater and more powerful than we will ever be on our own. Satan is the problem, and Satan is the one who deceived us with the lies and false perceptions of what our reality actually was. Satan was also the one who then increased the manipulations in an effort to keep us going down that fateful path. And Satan is the one who lied to us once again, filling us with the shame of believing that we weren't succeeding at life because we just aren't good enough.

We alone cannot defeat Satan and the ways of this world. Satan has powers and abilities that we as human beings are unable to fathom. Satan, before he turned to sin and rebellion, was one of the most powerful angels in heaven. A mighty spiritual force equaled by only a few. For us to think that we alone can overpower or outsmart him is absolutely ludicrous. Yet in our naivety many of us think that we can. And just as foolish are those who believe that if they ignore and refuse to acknowledge the existence of Satan in their lives, he won't be a factor.

Fortunately for us, we were created by a God that loves us more than anything He ever created. And despite our choice to turn away from Him, deny Him, and ignore Him; He still desires nothing more than to be in a close, personal, and intimate relationship with each and every one of us. God was well aware that Satan would not hold anything back in his attacks upon us. God also knew that in and of ourselves we would never be able to overcome Satan. Therefore, out of His love and desire to be with us, God planned for this in the crucifixion and resurrection of His Son, Jesus Christ.

Jesus Christ overcame Satan and sin when He walked in this world as a man. Jesus Christ overcame death and the bondage that Satan holds us in when He was resurrected from the grave. Jesus Christ said to each and every one of us –

"I will not say much more to you, for the prince of this world is coming. He has no hold over me." John 14:30

"Very truly I tell you, whoever believes in me will do the works I have been doing, and they will do even greater things than these, because I am going to the Father." John 14:12

"On that day you will realize that I am in my Father, and you are in me, and I am in you." John 14:20

Once we accept Jesus Christ as our Lord and Savior, we live in Christ and for Christ. We are one with Christ. Therefore, in being one with Christ, we receive the powers and abilities of Christ, thru Him. In Christ, we can overcome Satan and defeat the powers of darkness. In Christ we can and will do so much more than we believe we are capable of. I know for many of you this may be a bit difficult to grasp right now, but don't worry, it will become more clear as you strengthen your relationship with Christ. This too is Satan, working to keep us from knowing the truth and who we truly were created to be.

The New You

We have spent most of our time in this the book realizing the traits and tendencies of the poser; those undesirable qualities which we long to leave behind. For the remainder of this chapter, we'll take a peek at what lies ahead for us in our return to the person we were created to be. We'll get a glimpse of what is in store for us and build an understanding of what that life may look like.

Our new life, which I refer to as 'new' as most of us have no recollection of its prior existence, will and must be centered around God and Jesus Christ.

In the world that we live in hierarchy is commonplace. We are taught from a very young age that an implied 'pecking order' exists within our societies. The term 'pecking order' was derived from the Dominance Hierarchy whereby one's status in a society was determined by their dominance over others. The one with the greatest status would be at the top of that order and the one with the least at the bottom. The one with higher status in the order would receive more benefits, rights, opportunities, privileges, and so on.

Regardless of social class and/or financial status, every single one of us has accepted this societal norm. Therefore, regardless of our position in that 'pecking order', each of us *looks up to* and *down upon* others depending on the status level that WE have assigned to these others. Yes, believe it or not, it is a value that we ourselves place upon others based solely on our perspective; most always being based entirely on how we view ourselves and not how we view the other person. Yes, that is correct! How we view ourselves! One may think that is backwards, but then again, many of our perceptions of this world are backwards.

The fundamental truth is that you are you, and I am me. I, nor anyone else, can determine or tell you who you are or what you can or cannot achieve. That can only be done by you. You are the only one who gets to choose whether you are a success or a failure. We could start a whole 'nother book on this issue, but for now we will leave it with the basic perception of our social hierarchy.

Nonetheless, there is an order in life that we all follow and subscribe too. I'm sure you know your place, or where you are perceived to be in the circle of people that you associate with. And as we just stated, this positioning is solely determined by the perspective of each individual. You could put ten people into a group and have each one compile a list of the other nine from strongest to weakest and you would get ten different responses. These 'status' levels that we place upon others do not change anything in life other than the ways in which we view ourselves.

This all goes back to Chapter 5, and our discussion on *The Wounds*. Our perspective and understanding of matters become damaged and fragmented over time causing us to see things in a way that is not consistent with reality. Our perspective and understanding is also formed by our past experiences and at no time can that perspective or understanding be any greater than the extent of what we have allowed ourselves to take in. In other words – My perspective and understanding will never be able to rationalize or comprehend someone or something that I have not experienced myself. We are all limited by the depth of what we have allowed ourselves to experience and take in.

Furthermore, since we attempt to rationalize everyone and everything that we encounter, all of our endeavors to do so will base these assumptions on how we have come to view matters ourselves. Essentially, we try to assimilate everything that we encounter with something in our past that we have experienced and are able to understand. We bring most everything down to our level so that it will make sense to us.

We do this same thing with God and Jesus as well. We have all heard tales about them, both good and bad. Maybe you attend a church or read the Bible. Maybe you already have a relationship with God and Jesus. Either way, it is likely questionable whether the perceptions which we hold of God and Jesus Christ are an accurate reflection of who they truly are.

More than likely, in all of our efforts and experiences, we dumb down God and Jesus as well, to a level that we can understand and make sense of. I don't say this to insult anyone's intelligence, understanding, faith, or relationship with God. This is simply who we are as human beings, and the way that our brain works. We attempt to rationalize or make sense of everything that we encounter.

It is in this process to understand that we bring all matters down to our own level of comprehension.

When our perspective becomes properly aligned with the true character of God and Jesus Christ, a whole new world opens up for us. Not only do we begin to see and understand the true fullness of God and His greatness, but we also begin to see life and the world which we live in from His perspective as well. Our focus, our priority, our primary reason for living now revolves around God and Jesus Christ. If our primary focus is on God, everything in and around our lives then gets viewed through that perspective.

So how are we supposed to obtain a correct perspective of God and Jesus Christ, and become aligned with their will and desires, when they are nothing like any experience that we may have had in the past?

This, my friends, is the easy part. All you have to do is show up! Yep – just like we mentioned earlier, you just keep showing up and showing God that you truly seek Him and desire him with all of your heart. You keep showing up in prayer, in communication, seeking advice and direction, and asking for His wisdom and will. As long as it's done with true intention and from the heart, God will always be there and God will always answer. And over time, God will show you who He truly is as well as who you truly were created to be.

When our views become aligned with that of God, and His will, our life gets back on the track that we were created to roll down. This alignment, or union with God, brings us into His favor and blessings. Not to say that God does not bless or allow things to happen for those who are not in union with Him, but for those who are a whole new world and way of life is exposed.

Here is an oversimplified allegory that may make this a bit more under-standable:

I have a friend that lives down the street from me. Generally speaking, he is what most would call a 'good 'ole boy'. He is respectful, honest, trustworthy, hardworking, and will most always go out of his way to help others. We have a good relationship. While I wouldn't say that we are best friends, we do hang out together, golf together, and occasionally take our wives out for a night on the town together. My friend and his family also join us at our house for BBQ's, holiday gatherings, and other get-togethers. We know them well and they know us well. I believe that I have even gone as far as saying that "my house is his house", and his family is welcome at our house anytime.

I also have a son. My pride and joy. He is a spitting image of me and wants to be just like his dad. He is still a teenager and oftentimes will do the foolish things that teenage boys do. But he is learning, trying, and quick to accept and correct the mistakes that he makes. I can tell that he always desires to please his dad, although his actions may not always reflect it. I love my son more than life itself and would do anything for him. My biggest pleasure in life is seeing him happy, enjoying what he is doing. I go out of my way to try and bring this joy and happiness into his life.

I have worked hard all of my life and have been fortunate enough to accumulate a tidy sum of money, a good-sized home, and many other treasures and valuables. This is my life, this is my domain, this is my blood, sweat, and tears. It is what I have placed value upon due to the effort required of me in obtaining these things.

While I do allow my neighbor friend access to my family and my home, he does not have full access. He is limited on what he is allowed to see, do, and partake in. He is not family, and these privileges can and will be revoked at any time should an offense occur that would warrant so.

My son, on the other hand, is family. He knows everything about our family – things that will never be shared with those outside of our family. He shares in everything that I have and enjoys the spoils of things that I seek out just for him. He knows where the keys to the safe are and where all of our valuables are stored. He also knows that he is loved unconditionally, and that this will never change, regardless of what mistakes he may make in life.

That son, my son, is who each of us are in Christ. God is the Father that wants to pour out all of the blessings of His kingdom upon us, His children. And while we may screw up from time to time, we are loved unconditionally, regardless. This is the truth that we need to live in. This is the God, our Father, that we need to learn about and know. We wholeheartedly need to learn who we are as a child of God. Once we begin to understand our position in the family of God our perspective on all things will change dramatically, and a whole new world will open up to us. We need to stop listening to who and what the world says God is and turn to God Himself with our questions and uncertainties.

In realigning our perspective of God, we will surely begin to see His goodness, along with His love and desire for us. We must not be confused, however. Knowing who God is and knowing God are not the same thing, and do not offer the same benefits. A large majority of Christians today have accepted Jesus Christ as their Savior, ensuring their salvation, but do not know God or Christ. They have been adopted into the family of God and will be with Christ in heaven at some point in time.

However, this is one of the biggest faults or shortcomings of the modern church as well as modern day Christians. We lead others to Christ, for their salvation, and then they are on their own. They know who God is and have committed to follow Him, but they aren't shown how to have a close intimate relationship with God and Christ. Yes, they will get to heaven; but they will not live the life that God had intended for them, and that He so desperately desires to bless us with.

Our salvation, accepting Christ as our Lord and Savior, is just the beginning. It is only the ticket that gets you into the front gate of the theme park. There is so much more past the front gate, and nobody ever goes to a theme park just to stand inside of the gates. They go for the experience. They go for the thrills. They go for the adventure. They go for the fun, the joy, the happiness, the excitement. And they also go for the unknown. The unknown feeling of your stomach coming up through your throat as you are dropped in a sling from a platform some hundred feet up. The unknown feeling of your brain being scrambled as you fly through the corkscrew upside down on the rollercoaster. And the many other unknown feelings that they dive into without any forethought.

This is how we need to look at our acceptance of Christ as well. He is just our ticket in. Lucky for us though, He will also be our guide through the park. Leading us on the best rides, the biggest adventures, and the most memorable experiences – as long as we stay with Him. There is so much more than our salvation. And no one that has ever ventured past the front gate has ever come back asking for a refund.

The Bible undoubtedly confirms that God's love, grace, and mercies are unconditional. Even those who do not believe in God are loved by Him. God also gives mercy and grace to those non-believers as well. We need not do anything to receive these three things from God. Once we accept Christ as our Lord and Savior however, the love, grace, and mercy are abounded.

However, to live our life to the fullest, to be that person that we were created and intended to be, requires us to maintain a constant and ongoing relationship with God and Christ. And as with any worldly relationship that we may have, it requires constant effort, communication, attention, and desire on our part for that relationship to flourish. Yes, we have to work at it. But just as with all of the other pleasures in our lives, if we want or desire something bad enough, we find a way to put forth the time and effort.

All of the other blessings and provisions that God has planned for us are conditional. The condition of our desire for Him and our relationship with Him. Once we begin to seek and desire God intimately, and truly from our hearts, that whole new world begins to open up and we are able to experience our life as a son or daughter of a true King.

If you are like me, you probably tried to assimilate the depth of that last statement through your own reasoning and experiences. For me, with my background and the wounds which I had received, it came down to 'work'. I grew up believing the lie that I had to work harder and better to prove myself. That it was only through my work and efforts that I would receive anything. And that the quality and extent of my work determined who and what I was, as well as what and how much I would receive. So automatically, my mind went straight to the thought of having to perform or work to a certain standard or level to have this relationship with God.

This was how I attempted to comprehend God – through the understanding of my past experiences.

That, again, is not who God is. While partaking in those other 'benefits and blessings' is conditional and does require effort on our part, it is only in the effort of seeking to strengthen and grow our relationship with God that we must work. God will do the rest, and He will even strengthen us along the way to help us succeed.

We need to relearn who we are as God's children and who that person is that we were created to be. In doing so, we need only listen to the Creator, God, our Father, and what He says we are and should be. God's perspective and opinion is the only one that matters, and the only one which we should desire to align ourselves with. We should wholeheartedly desire to pursue God and His desires for our life instead of chasing after what we believe the world asks of us.

Let people feel the weight of who you are as a child of God and let them deal with it.

"As for God, his way is perfect: The Lord's word is flawless; he shields all who take refuge in him." 2 Samuel 22:31

Chapter 19

Football?

We've learned a lot about ourselves and our life as a poser in the first eighteen chapters. I'm hoping that your awareness has been enhanced, even if only in the slightest bit, to the fact that our perspective and perception of all things are greatly flawed. I also hope that you have come to realize that our flawed perception and perspective are intentional and are just one of the many weapons used to keep us from reaching our true potential.

It is in the way that we see things, and then the way that we perceive those matters, which shapes and molds not only who we are, but our direction in life as well. A perfect example of this truth unfolded over the past five months, playing out on National television, for the whole world to see.......... if you were paying attention.

I understand that a chapter on College Football may not seem to fall in line with the rest of this book, especially relating to the life of a poser. Football, however, is only the backdrop for this story. As you will come to see, how we perceive things affects not only us, but also has the power to affect a multitude of others around us as well.

I love College Football and closely follow the season, the teams, and the games every year. I was born and raised in Nebraska, home of the Cornhuskers. Nebraska is not a highly populated state; therefore, we don't have any professional sports teams. If you grow up in Nebraska, or have any ties to Nebraska, more than likely the Huskers are your team.

I got hooked on Nebraska football at a very young age. Probably due to the fact that during this time of my life, the 1970's, Nebraska was a dominant powerhouse year after year. Having won the National Championship in 1970 and 1971, Nebraska continued to remain a force and was the third or fourth ranked team for that decade. The 1971 team is considered to be one of the best that ever played the game, finishing the season with a perfect 13-0 record, and defeating #2 Oklahoma in what is often referred to as 'The Game of The Century'.

College football is real. It's young men showing up every day just to earn a chance. Young men giving it their all, to be the best that they can be. Young men fighting till the very last minutes of the game, no matter what the score may be.

A rather astonishing event played out in College Football this year. One that shocked the entire world. An event that made everyone step back in awe while saying *"There has to be something more going on here"*.
That event – The Indiana Hoosiers won the National Championship and finished the season with a perfect 16-0 record.

Now to many of you this may appear to be no big deal. It's just another team. Somebody had to win it all. Why not them? And given enough chances, maybe they just got lucky. Ya, that might be what it looked like to the outsider, but there is a whole lot more to this story than just another team winning the National Championship.

The Hoosier's story of their 2025 season brings to mind James 4:10, which says: *"Humble yourselves before the Lord, and he will lift you up."*

Leading into the 2025 season the Indiana Hoosiers were one of the worst teams in the history of college football. They had lost more than seven hundred games; more than any other team in the 156 years of college football. So how is it possible to go from the worst to the best in less than two years? Obviously, many things had to perfectly fall into place. Albeit none of these things were significant enough to transform the entire team............. except for one.

The first major event in Indiana's conversion was the hiring of a new Head Coach. As with most Colleges and Universities, if an athletic program is not winning, that Head Coach can pretty much be assured that he or she will soon be replaced. Having an athletic program with a winning record brings a substantial amount of money into that college or university, not to mention the national recognition and publicity, which then draws in even greater talent as well as more students who now desire to attend that school. The higher a team is ranked in the National rankings, the more the school benefits.... exponentially.

The football program at most schools, along with its coaching staff, bears the majority of this burden. The football program at most schools brings in most all of the funds for that athletic department, and more often than not, enables the funding of other programs within that school. The success of a college football team, or lack thereof, can often make or break the College or University itself.

In November of 2023, Indiana hired Curt Cignetti to be the new Head Coach of their football team. Cignetti was no stranger to college football. He began his career as a graduate assistant at Pittsburgh from 1983-84, and then coached at Davidson, Rice, and Temple. He then moved to NC State as a recruiting coordinator and quarterbacks/tight ends coach from 2000-2006. A solid beginning to a coaching career, albeit with smaller schools and insignificant teams.

The first big break in Cignetti's career came in 2007, when he was hired as the recruiting coordinator and wide receivers coach under Nick Saban for the

University of Alabama. Cignetti contributed to the early stages of the Alabama dynasty by recruiting key players such as Mark Ingram. Ingram went on to win the Heisman trophy in 2009 and helped lead Alabama to National Champions.

Cignetti had proven his abilities and was now beginning to grab the attention of other schools as a possible candidate for the position of Head Coach. In 2011, Cignetti was hired by Indiana University of Pennsylvania (IUP). As their head coach, he compiled a 53-17 record over six seasons. Cignetti then moved to Elon University from 2017–2018 as their head coach, leading the team to two FCS playoff appearances.

The next big break for Cignetti came in 2019 when he was offered the position of Head Coach with James Madison University. As head coach, he went 52-9, winning four conference championships and leading the team in its transition from FCS to FBS, and finishing 11-1 in 2023. The differences between an FCS team and an FBS team are significant. While an FCS team is still Division I football; the perks, benefits, scholarships, pay, and talent are much less than that of an FBS team. It would be much like the minor leagues of college football.

An FBS team is where everyone wants to play, and coach. Cignetti had now made it to the top position on a Division I FBS team. And even though JMU was not a name that would make people stand up and take notice, Cignetti was now in the 'big leagues' and would soon have a much bigger set of eyes looking upon him.

In his first fifteen years of coaching, Cignetti had built a solid reputation as a 'turnaround specialist' and an exceptional recruiter. Exactly the skills that Colleges and Universities are looking for when things aren't going their way.

During the 2023 season, Indiana finished with a 3-9 record. They finished dead last in the Big 10 conference having won only one conference game. That was enough for their Athletic Director. It was time to look for that change, which came soon after in the hiring of Cignetti at the end of the 2023 season.

Cignetti continued to do what he does best in his first season with Indiana, taking them to their first-ever 10-win season, and reaching the College Football Playoffs (CFP) for the first time. The 2024 Indiana Hoosiers football team was exceptionally good, finishing their season ranked #10 in the final AP poll with an 11-2 record. They set program records for wins, conference wins (8-1), and national ranking under their new coach, making it a landmark, Cinderella-like season for the program despite a first-round CFP loss to Notre Dame.

The 2024 season alone would have been miraculous by college football standards. Going from a 3-win season in 2023 to a top 10 ranking the next. However, Cignetti knew something that the good people of Indiana did not but would soon find out.

The 2025 season began and while Cignetti was pleased, he was far from satisfied. He saw more, much more. If only he could get everyone else to see what he could see.

Just as any coach does, Cignetti continued to recruit. Always attempting to find the right talent and the right person for each position. The difficulty with this, however, is that no one wants to go play football for a team that is known as being the worst in the country. No one with much talent or potential anyways. Cignetti knew this already, as he had been facing that challenge all of his career. What Cignetti did was learn to look at any potential recruits not for the talent that they already possessed, but to look at their character and their potential, which was often overlooked by other programs.

Turning any college football program around requires athletes with exceptional talent and ability, especially at the Division I level. You can have the best coaches in the country, but if the boys can't play worth a lick, it's all for nothing. We know that Cignetti was an excellent recruiter. We also know that no big named players with talent would come to Indiana. Cignetti did recruit though and brought many new players into the program. Towards the end of the 2025 season, an ESPN analyst stated the following about the entire team of Indiana Hoosiers:

"They have no 5-star players. Nobody stands out above the others. What they do have is a team, a team of young men all working together for the same goal, with the same understanding."

One of those recruits brought in was a Junior from the University of California named Fernando Mendoza. Mendoza was a quarterback and had been all of his playing career. He had a somewhat successful run as the QB on his High School team but was never recruited by any of the top colleges. Mendoza had settled on the fact that he would have to get a degree and then go on to the business world after college. And if he was lucky – he might be able to play on the football team while he was there.

Mendoza initially decided to attend Yale University for his Business degree, but later flipped to the University of California, Berkeley. Mendoza red-shirted as a Freshman on the California Bears team in 2022. He didn't earn his first start until the sixth game of the following year. Mendoza then earned the starting spot as QB for the Bears for the remainder of the 2023 season and the entirety of the 2024 season. At the end of the 2024 season, Mendoza declared that he would be entering the 'transfer portal'.

The transfer portal is a new system within college football where players can now put themselves 'up for transfer' if another school is willing to accept them. Another benefit of this system is that these players can now play on the new team immediately. Prior transfers had to sit out for a year before being eligible to play.

I don't know exactly what was running through Cignetti's mind when he first looked at Mendoza, but I'm sure it did not involve basing his decision on Mendoza's past stats or performance. While Mendoza has many great qualities, he is....... let's say, awkward. You don't look at Mendoza and say, *"There's the next*

Peyton Manning". Sure, he has talent and ability. But you must understand that in Division I football, especially at the higher levels, everything is much bigger, much faster, and hurts a heck of a lot more when it hits you. Most guys fold quicker than a lawn chair when thrown into this environment. And Mendoza, while he was good, had never proven that he could hold up under pressure.

Nonetheless, Cignetti accepted the transfer. Mendoza would be the starting QB for Indiana in 2025. Cignetti also brought in several other transfers, each one being less impressive than Mendoza. Cignetti assembled his coaching staff in the same manner. No outstanding resumes. No superstars. Just a bunch of hard-working guys with character and potential. The Hoosiers would soon after refer to themselves as *"just a bunch of misfits with a place to call home"*.

At the start of the 2025 season, nobody was expecting much out of the Indiana Hoosiers. Why would they? There was nothing impressive about them and half the team had changed from their record-breaking season of last year. More than likely, Indiana was just another team that other teams saw on their schedule which would guarantee them one more win.

Indiana started the season with three wins over Old Dominion, Kennesaw State, and Indiana State. Boring!! Still not enough to sound off any alarms. Their fourth game was against Illinois. Illinois has potential, at least when they decide to show up. It is always 'hit or miss' with Illinois, and apparently this week Illinois missed. Week five brought Iowa. Now there is a game. Actually, it was a game where anyone would expect Iowa to dominate the entire game. Indiana wins 20-15.

Week six brought Indiana to play the #2 team in the country, the Oregon Ducks, in Oregon. Last weeks game against Iowa may have been a fluke. It surely wasn't enough to raise any eyebrows. When the Hoosiers outscored Oregon by 10 points on their home field, the whole country stood up and noticed. Indiana was now under the microscope with everyone trying to figure out why. How were they able to win these games? Who was it on the team that stood out? What made them better? All the answers were the same – Nobody knew why. There was nothing special about the Indiana Hoosiers. Nothing stood out!

Then came Michigan State, UCLA, and Maryland for another win, win, win. Nine games, nine wins. Week ten brought the Penn State Nittany Lions. Penn State had recently made it up to the #2 ranked team in the country as well but had lost a couple games and were dropping. Indiana happily handed them another loss and any chance for a ticket to the CFP playoffs with a 27-24 win.

Indiana finished off their regular season with resounding wins over Wisconsin and Purdue. Indiana finished the regular season with a record of 12-0, standing alone at the top of their side of the Big 10 Conference and moving them on to the Big 10 Conference Championship. This would be the first time in school history that Indiana achieved twelve wins.

The Big 10 Conference Championship would pit Indiana, who had now moved up in the rankings to the #2 spot, against Ohio State and their #1 ranking. Regardless of the outcome of the game, both teams would be moving on to the College Football Playoffs. Indiana played tough the entire game, never giving in and never looking like they didn't belong. Being in the same conference, Indiana and Ohio State have played each other many times over the years, with Indiana always being the proverbial 'little brother' who was constantly being reminded of his inferior place in life.

That was what everyone expected yet once again. That Indiana's perception of the bigger, stronger, and faster Ohio State would lead the Hoosiers into mentally defeating themselves. The Hoosiers had learned something new, however. They had become aware of what the truth actually was. And that truth led them to a 13-10 win in one of the best Conference Championship games ever played.

Indiana was now the Big 10 Champions. This, however, was not a first for Indiana who also won the title in 1945 and 1967. What was a first for the Hoosiers was that they were now the #1 ranked team in the country. With that #1 ranking, they would receive a bye through the first round of the playoffs and would not have to play another game for several weeks.

Another highlight of this season came during the off weeks while awaiting the playoffs. College Football rewards several players each year for their outstanding performance. There are several awards for both offensive and defensive players, with the most prestigious of these awards being the Heisman Trophy. The Heisman Trophy is awarded annually to the most outstanding college football player in the United States. It recognizes superior athletic ability, diligence, perseverance, and hard work. While The Heisman is often awarded to offensive positions, it is intended for any player whose performance best exemplifies overall excellence.

Fernando Mendoza, the awkward QB who went unacknowledged by every other team in the country, was nominated for the Heisman. By this point in Mid-December, it was very clear and evident who would be holding the trophy at the end of the night. To no one's surprise, Fernando Mendoza was recognized as the player with the best performance and ability throughout the year. Mendoza was also the first player in Indiana history to win the prestigious award.

Several weeks later, Indiana began their bid for the National Championship against Alabama, the team which Cignetti coached for several years. The playoffs are often highly anticipated, by both players and fans, as they involve the top teams who are playing their best. You are certain to be entertained by a good match-up in almost every game.

This, however, was not the case in this game. Alabama had easily beaten their first-round opponent to move on to the quarter finals and Indiana. Indiana received their bye into the quarter finals by way of their #1 ranking. The #2, #3, and #4 teams also received a bye into the quarter finals. All four of these teams had nearly three weeks of down time before their quarter final game, while their opponents were coming off of a win the prior week in the first round.

The #2, #3, and #4 teams had already played their quarter final game before Indiana and Alabama played – and all three had lost. Things were not looking good for the team that was supposed to be rested and ready to go. Maybe the extended layoff allowed them to become lazy and not sharp. Nonetheless, Indiana had to play and play they did. Indiana went on to route Alabama 38-3 in a very one-sided game.

The semi-finals would lead Indiana back to an old foe, Oregon. Oregon's only loss this season came to Indiana in that sixth game of the regular season when they were ranked #2 and touted to be the only serious competition for Ohio State. This would surely be a test for Indiana. After all, Oregon had already played them and knew what they were up against. They were prepared, so one would think.

In perfect Cignetti style, Indiana kept Oregon on their toes the entire first half, constantly mixing up plays and running the unexpected. The game was close at halftime and left everyone thinking that this just might be the undoing of the Hoosiers. But the second half came around, and Indiana showed a whole 'nother side that no one was expecting. Final score: Indiana 56 Oregon 22.

Only one game remained. The National Championship. Indiana would face Miami at *Hard Rock Stadium* in Miami, their home field. Miami had earned their way into the playoffs through a highly disputed 'pick' of the committee which had to choose between three teams all vying for the last spot, and all having two losses in the regular season. Miami had stepped up though and handily beaten all of their opponents in the first three rounds of the playoff.

I am sure you know the story by now. Indiana wins the National Championship, their first ever. They go on to have a perfect 16-0 season and set multiple records for the school and several players. Fernando Mendoza wins the coveted Heisman and is now projected to be the #1 pick in the first round of the NFL draft this year.

Another note of importance is that during each and every playoff game, all of which took place at venues halfway across the country, Indiana fans filled the stadiums often outnumbering the fans of the opposing team 5 to 1. At *Hard Rock Stadium* in Miami, Indiana fans compiled roughly 80% of the crowd, at Miami's home field.

So how was all of this possible? How were a bunch of 'misfits' able to compete at the highest level, and do so in such a dominant fashion? Remember – there was nothing extraordinary about any one of the players or the coaches. At least not until Curt Cignetti got ahold of them.

So, what made Cignetti so special? What is it that he did that brought about the miraculous? Well, actually, it's a couple things.

First, Cignetti knew what his priorities were, and he never wavered from them. His first priority is God, followed only by family and then football. With his first priority being God, Curt knew that man and man alone cannot achieve the impossible. That can only be done with a sincere belief and faith in God and what God can do.

Tied in with that belief, Curt knew that even with that belief and faith, a man will never reach his true potential until he fully realizes who he is in Christ. If man keeps listening to and believing what the world says he is, that man will never amount to anything.

When Cignetti first arrived at Indiana University, his first thought was not to recruit or rework the football team, or its staff. Curt's first thought was

Indiana, specifically the town of Bloomington. Bloomington Indiana has a population of roughly 85,000 people, of which nearly 45,000 are students at Indiana University.

Now, think back to the beginning of this chapter – Indiana was and always has been the most losing program in college football history. For over 156 years that is all the people of Indiana have known. That is what they expect. That is how they see and perceive the Indiana Hoosier football team. Those same players from that team are immersed into that environment every single day of their lives. They are not expected to win. They are not expected to do the miraculous. They are not seen by anyone with the ability to perform at a higher level.

Well, not until Curt Cignetti walked in. Curt knew that the first thing he had to do was change the perception of not only the football team, but of the residents of Indiana as well. He had to get everyone to see the players as winners. And then he had to get the players to see it themselves and fully believe that this is who they were. He had to get them to stop listening to what everyone else said they were and start believing in what God says they are.

Obviously, it was easier for Curt to get the football team on board with this perspective than it was the state. But Curt knew that if the players believed it, the state would soon follow close behind, which would only further push the players to be their best.

Curt Cignetti asked Fernando Mendoza a question before bringing him to Indiana. That question – *"How good do you want to be?"* Fernando answered him by saying *"I want to be the best QB in the country"*. Cignetti's reply was as to be expected from a man with his viewpoint – *"I don't know if you will become the best QB in the country, but I will surely make you the best QB that you can be!"*

Curt Cignetti knew that our perception of matters, as well as who we are, has a major impact on who we become and whether we reach our full potential or not. Curt knew he had good players, and he knew that those good players could be great players if they simply believed in themselves and stopped letting the world define who they were. All Curt did was remove the roadblocks, and then fine tune that natural ability that his players had, while keeping them on track and focused on their goal.

Hopefully this has been a valuable lesson for many of you. It is in our perspective and perceptions that we limit our own potential. It is the garbage, the lies, the deceptions, which we allow ourselves to believe that keep us from becoming the person that God created us to be. If we remain in Christ, and listen to what He says about us, we can truly be anything. It is on our own, in that self-life, the life of the poser, that we are always trying to be something else, something that will never amount to much at all.

"For I know the plans I have for you," declares the Lord, "plans to prosper you and not to harm you, plans to give you hope and a future." Jeremiah 29:11

Chapter 20

Returning Home

I am hopefully optimistic that through this book your eyes have been opened to the self-life that each of us has become so enamored with. It is also my hope that you have come to realize this self-life is nowhere near what our true potential is, or the life that we could be living.

For those who have made the commitment to follow the suggested steps and leave the life of the poser behind – Kudos to you! It will not be an easy process, but the reward will be more than worth your efforts. I strongly recommend going back and re-reading each of the steps every now and then just to make sure you are staying on course. There will be many attempts to derail you in this process and keep you from returning to that person you were created to be. These attacks will come on stronger and harder than ever before, all coming from the kingdom of darkness. As long as we remain in Christ, we have no reason to fear these attacks as we now have the powers and authority through Christ to overcome anything.

For those who are not quite ready to abandon the comforts and bondage of their life as a poser, I am grateful that you have at least allowed yourself to read the entire book and I am hoping that your awareness of a greater life may have increased, even if only in the slightest bit. True knowledge is power, and it will lead you to the life that you were meant to live.

Our True Home

Once we begin to appreciate who we are in Christ, as well as our position in the family of God, it will become very evident to us that we are not a part of this world. This new comprehension will lead us to realize that we were created for something much greater than this world can offer, and that our true home is with God and Jesus in a heavenly realm.

Jesus tells us in John 14:20: *"On that day you will realize that I am in my Father, and you are in me, and I am in you."*

Jesus Christ was crucified, died, and was buried in the tomb. On the third day he rose again and ascended into heaven. Jesus tells us that if we are in Him, having accepted Him as our Lord and Savior, then He is in us as well. Therefore, since Christ is already seated at the right hand of God, we are as well as we are in Christ. Our home, our citizenship, is in Heaven and in Christ we are already there. We are merely visitors in this world, and it would benefit each of us to firmly hold this truth as a core belief.

In Ephesians 1, Paul tells us: *"[18]I pray that the eyes of your heart may be enlightened in order that you may know the hope to which he has called you, the riches of his glorious inheritance in his holy people, [19]and his incomparably great power for us who believe. That power is the same as the mighty strength [20]he exerted when he raised Christ from the dead and seated him at his right hand in the heavenly realms, [21]far above all rule and authority, power and dominion, and every name that is invoked, not only in the present age but also in the one to come."*

Incomparably great power for us who believe! The same power that He exerted when He raised Christ from the dead. Paul is talking about the power of the Holy Spirit, the Spirit of God, which dwells within every believer. Paul is praying that we may be enlightened so to become aware of this power within us. In a sense – Paul is praying that the veil of darkness be lifted from our eyes and our hearts so that we may see past the lies and deceptions that keep us from knowing this truth.

This power, the Holy Spirit of God, is God. It is the power of God, and it dwells within us. I am sure that many of you may be wondering: *"If this power is within me, then why do I not feel all powerful?"*

The simple answer is faith. It is a lack or non-existence of our faith. The power IS within us. The problem is that we simply don't believe in these powers or that we have these powers as again we have chosen to accept the lies and deceptions and the understanding of this world as our reality.

Jesus tells us in Matthew 17:20: *"Because you have so little faith. Truly I tell you, if you have faith as small as a mustard seed, you can say to this mountain, 'Move from here to there,' and it will move. Nothing will be impossible for you."*

I also find it rather significant that three verses earlier in 17:17, Jesus says: *"You unbelieving and perverse generation, how long shall I stay with you? How long shall I put up with you?"*

This rebuke from Jesus came shortly after the disciples had unsuccessfully tried to heal a demon possessed child with their powers which they had recently become aware of.

Our beliefs become our reality. If we are unable to fundamentally believe something to our core, that something will never become a part of our reality or who we truly are. While the disciples may have understood Jesus when He gave them powers, they did not truly hold a belief that this was who they were. It is also quite possible that they may have possessed a 'half-hearted' belief as well, thinking *"it would be cool if we had those powers, but I don't know how to do any of that stuff."*

Therein lies the problem with these powers, as well as many of the other claims and promises made to us by God and Jesus. It is yet again our perspective of the matter. We as mankind do not hold these special powers or abilities. It is Jesus who holds them. However, since we are 'in Christ' just as He is 'in us', we have access to those powers and abilities through Christ. Without Christ we are nothing more than the pile of sludge that we were before.

Another major roadblock that keeps us from reaching our full potential and becoming that person we were created to be lies with our perspective of where we are from. In Chapter 2, we mentioned the quote from W. Clement Stone – *"We are all a product of our own environment."*

For us, we were born into this world, we reside in this world, and we live out every part of our lives in this world. The world that we live in has become our environment. Therefore, what we have become is a product of this world as it is what we see, feel, experience, and know. To us, it is home. It is what we know and where we exist.

The reality of our existence is that we are not of this world. We are from the Kingdom of Heaven, or the Kingdom of God. This is our true home, our true environment. This is where we were created and where we will return too when God calls each of us home. For most of us, however, we do not make this home our true environment. Just as us posers do, we like to hang out in an environment that we were not created or intended for. We believe that everything around us is our true environment, and therefore we adapt and allow that environment to change us.

Since we are all a product of our own environment, it would be safe to assume that if we change our environment, what and who we are would then change as well. Once we learn to accept that our true home is not in this world, that our citizenship actually lies elsewhere, the entire process of changing our environment becomes rather simple.

Once we have accepted the reality of that citizenship, we then immerse ourselves in that world and that environment. We do this through constant prayer and communication with our Father and Jesus Christ. It is through this prayer and communication that we will be drawn closer to God and His will, and which His will and desires then become ours. God will then lead us to all of the worldly things that He wishes for us to do, but we will now be doing these things because we desire to please our Father, not ourselves.

This simple change in our perspective about where we truly live will completely change our environment, as well as how we see ourselves and how others see us too.

We should also be aware that this change in our beliefs and thinking does not happen overnight. It takes effort, intention, and practice. The biggest step that we can make towards learning these new truths is to stop listening to what the world says about us and what the world wants us to hear (social media, news outlets, television, and anyone in your life that is not lifting you up or encouraging you) and start listening to what God and Jesus say about us.

Don't forget – 90% or more of what we see, hear, and experience every single day is not what it appears to be. However, each and every bit of it is intentional and has a purpose and rarely is that purpose for our benefit.

Weapons

As we have discussed in previous chapters, we are smack dab in the middle of a war. The war between good and evil. And just like any other war – our Great Commander has given us the tools and weapons we need to fight the battles which we are called to fight. Keep in mind, however, just because we have these weapons does not mean that every battle is ours to fight. Since we are now in constant communication with Jesus and God, they will let us know which battles are ours and which ones to walk away from.

The Apostle Paul tells us in 2 Corinthians 10:4 – *"The weapons we fight with are not the weapons of the world. On the contrary, they have divine power to demolish strongholds."*

Paul also tells us in Ephesians 6:10-12 – *"¹⁰Finally, be strong in the Lord and in his mighty power. ¹¹Put on the full armor of God, so that you can take your stand against the devil's schemes. ¹²For our struggle is not against flesh and blood, but against the rulers, against the authorities, against the powers of this dark world and against the spiritual forces of evil in the heavenly realms."*

Put on the full armor of God? What the heck is that and can we get it on Amazon? Again, we are thinking of something tangible, something that our mind can relate too. We need begin to think beyond what the world has taught us and allow ourselves to open our mind to something beyond our comprehension.

Paul continues on in Ephesians 6, explaining the Armor of God – *"¹⁴Stand firm then, with the belt of truth buckled around your waist, with the breastplate of righteousness in place, ¹⁵and with your feet fitted with the readiness that comes from the gospel of peace. ¹⁶In addition to all this, take up the shield of faith, with which you can extinguish all the flaming arrows of the evil one. ¹⁷Take the helmet of salvation and the sword of the Spirit, which is the word of God."*

Paul also adds one more item in verse 18 – *"¹⁸And pray in the Spirit on all occasions with all kinds of prayers and requests."*

Some of you may be curious as to who this Paul guy is that we keep quoting. Was he one of the twelve disciples that rarely got mentioned? Most of us are familiar with at least a few of the 'more popular' disciples. Matthew, Peter, John

– those are the easy ones. We have probably heard the idiom 'doubting Thomas', dubbed after Thomas the disciple. And if we know anything about Christianity, we are likely familiar with the 'Judas kiss' taken from the action that disciple Judas took to betray Jesus.

But what about Bartholomew or Thaddeus? Those are a couple of names you don't hear often, yet they were among the original twelve. If you guessed that Paul was NOT one of the twelve disciples, you are correct. Paul did not come into the picture until a few years after the crucifixion of Jesus – at least not as Paul. Paul was around prior to his life changing encounter with Christ, but he worked for the other side. Paul, who was previously known as Saul, went around persecuting Christians and the church. His sole purpose was to bring down any hope for expansion of the Christian church or its religion.

Then one day, on a somewhat routine trip to Damascus to seek out and torture Christians, Jesus himself appeared before Saul on the roadside. A truly divine encounter from God, which changed Saul's life forever, and changed him into Paul. Paul was hand-picked by God to spread the word of the gospel to the Gentiles.

Paul was almost immediately transformed by the presence of Christ. He had now seen and witnessed the Truth, the Way, and the Life. From this point on, Paul knew that there was only one way to go moving forward. That way was complete and total submission and service to Jesus Christ himself – out of love, respect, and gratefulness for what Jesus had done for us.

You can read the full story of Paul's encounter in the book of Acts. Paul would be right up near the top of the list of those that would be acceptable for us to imitate, likely being only second to Jesus himself.

Armor of God

So, what exactly is this Armor of God, and how do we use it? Well, depending on your source, the Armor of God consists of either six or seven items. The first six items are listed in Ephesians 6:14-17. The seventh item would be as Paul added in Ephesians 6:18, praying in the Spirit.

Let's go through each of the items individually to gain a better understanding of each one, and then we can add them to our new set of core beliefs.

Belt of truth –

Many of us have a belt, if not several. The primary purpose of wearing a belt is to keep our clothes from falling off. It firmly grips our clothing to our waistline, keeping them in place. The Belt of Truth does the same thing. It helps us to hold the rest of our armor in place and prevents it from falling away.

But this is no ordinary belt. It is the Belt of Truth. The truths of the gospel, the truths of our Father, the truths of Jesus Christ. It is the truths of who we are in Christ and as children of God. It is in knowing and believing these truths that we are able to stand firm against the attacks of darkness and this world. We are able to confidently resist the lies and deceptions as we fully know and believe what the truth is.

Another way in which the Belt of Truth strengthens us is by keeping us grounded in the truth, motivating us to live a life with honesty and integrity. When we know and believe what the truth is, that then becomes who we are.

Breastplate of righteousness –

The breastplate is the piece of armor that covers and protects our torso, or the main part of our body. The breastplate specifically covers and protects our heart. Proverbs 4:23 states: *"Above all else, guard your heart, for everything you do flows from it."*

So, what is a breastplate of righteousness? It is the righteousness of Jesus Christ that He gives to us freely. It is the protection through this righteousness of Christ which guards us from the attacks and accusations of Satan. And it is only through Christ that we can receive this righteousness.

Shoes of the gospel –

Paul tells us to stand firm with our feet fitted with the readiness that comes from the gospel of peace. When we put on these 'shoes' of the gospel, we are preparing ourselves to be ready with the gospel of peace. What is it that we are to be ready for? Well, as Paul highlights in verse 12, it is the attacks from the enemy, the rulers, the authorities, the powers of this dark world and the spiritual forces of evil in the heavenly realms.

Anger, fear, frustration, envy, and many other sinful emotions begin to overtake us when we choose to believe the lies and deceptions that are being hurled against us. It is the gospel of peace, the gospel of Jesus Christ, which keeps us grounded, obedient, and faithful to our loving Father.

Shield of faith -

The shield of faith – with which we can extinguish all flaming arrows of the evil one. The flaming arrows are the tools used by the evil one to attack us. No, they are not literally flaming arrows. Many times, they are simply a hurtful word or insult from another. These tools, or weapons, can come in any form, shape, or size. They most always will come when we least expect them though.

That is the evil one's plan – to attack us in a way that we are not prepared for and to do so when we are the least prepared for it. The sole intention is to catch us off guard, to make us slip up, to entice us into doing something that does not honor or glorify our Father. That is where the shield of faith comes in. It is in our faith – Our belief and confidence in God and who we are in Him – that we are prepared to defend these attacks, regardless of when or how they may happen. If we know who we truly are and what we truly believe in, no weapon formed against us will ever succeed.

Helmet of salvation -

The helmet of salvation – much like the belt of truth and the breastplate of righteousness, the helmet protects a vital part of our body as well. It protects our head, or our mind.

Paul tells us in Romans 7 that the battle begins in the mind. This is where Satan will begin his attacks, on our mind, on our thoughts. If Satan is able to control our mind, he then has full control over our body as well. And it all begins with simple little lies and deceptions in an effort to make us see or believe something in a way contrary to what it actually is.

The helmet protects our head, and our mind. However, this is no ordinary helmet. It is the helmet of salvation – our salvation. As a Christian, it is crucial that we fully understand exactly what the death of Jesus Christ meant and exactly what significance it has on our lives. If you aren't fully aware, I would strongly suggest that your next reading material be an in-depth study of the crucifixion, resurrection, and ascension of Jesus Christ so that you not only understand why all of this happened, but you also become aware of what it means for you as a Christian.

For now, we will focus only on the crucifixion, as it pertains to our salvation.

We are all sinners. From the time we are born, that is who we are. This goes back to the Garden of Eden, with Adam and Eve allowing sin to enter the world. We are all sinful by nature, choosing to walk away from God, our Creator. In this sin there is only death. No joy, no happiness, no peace. Nothing but a life, and a death, completely separated from God.

Even though we, as human beings, chose this path – it is not what God created us to be and certainly not what God wants or desires. God wants to be with each and every one of us. God wants to pour out His riches and blessings upon us. However, God cannot and will not tolerate sin. Therefore, there had to be an atonement for our sin. Something that would wipe away all of our sins, making us pure and holy in Gods sight.

That atonement, or sacrifice, was Jesus Christ. God sent his one and only Son to live in our world and face the same challenges and temptations that we do. The life Jesus lived was pure and holy, resisting all sin and temptation, and thereby conquering and defeating sin. Jesus was then crucified on the cross for crimes he did not commit and put to death. In this crucifixion and death, Jesus took on all the sin of every man, woman, and child; past, present, and future – so that we may be one with God, living in complete union with Him. If we have accepted Christ as our Savior, all of our sins have been forgiven; past, present, and future. They have been erased. We have been washed clean by the blood of Jesus Christ and that sacrifice.

This is our salvation. It is our redemption. It is the blood of Christ which has saved us from sin, from death, and from the enemy. We were purchased by the blood of Christ and now belong to Him. Satan no longer has a hold on us, and if we remain in Christ and His word and truths, Satan can no longer take hold of us either.

It is knowing who we are in Christ, through His sacrifice, that the helmet of salvation protects us.

An important note here – In Christ, all of our sins have been forgiven; past, present, and future. Most people are able to grasp the past and present indicators but have difficulty understanding the future implications. So, let's shed some light on our future sins so they don't cause us to stumble when they do happen.

One of our new core beliefs is that God is omniscient. Omniscient means *knowing everything or having unlimited understanding or knowledge.* God is the only one with this ability. God knew all things before He created this world, and before He created you and me. He knows every little detail of our lives, and exactly how they will play out. He knew every little sin that you and I committed in the past long before we even headed down that road. And just the same, He knows every sin that we will also commit in the future.

When Jesus gave His life on the cross, it was for the forgiveness of ALL sin. Therefore, if we have accepted Christ as our Lord and Savior, God has already forgiven us for our future sins which we aren't even aware of yet. However, if we have accepted Christ and are living in Him and through Him, we are expected to repent, or turn away from that sin, and turn back to Christ.

The key takeaway here is that in living our life for Christ we do not need to return to the bondage that Satan will surely pile upon us through shame for the sin that we have committed. We are free in Christ. Satan no longer has power or control over us so we don't need to live in that shame and guilt for the wrong that we have done. Once we repent and turn back to Christ – forget about it. That sin is not who we are, it is just something that we mistakenly did. It no longer defines who and what we are. Christ defines us. The cross defines us. And Christ and the cross have guaranteed our forgiveness forever!

Sword of the Spirit -
The sword of the Spirit is the word of God. It is God Himself living within us. It is His truths, His promises, and His covenants. It is His daily word that leads us and guides us in life. Remaining in these truths and promises, in God's word, protects us from falling victim to the lies and deceptions which bombard us every day.

Although Jesus was the son of God, he defeated the temptations of Satan during His forty days in the wilderness by using a weapon that everyone has at their disposal: the sword of the Spirit, which is the Word of God. Jesus countered all temptations from Satan, which were merely lies and deceptions, with scriptural truth.

Praying in the spirit –

Probably one of the most important tools we can have as a Christian. As we discussed previously, these tools, these powers, are not an ability which we have to conjure up on our own. They all come from Christ and through Christ. It is only by means of a close and intimate relationship with Christ that we have these powers. That close and intimate relationship only comes through constant communication – Prayer.

It should be evident by now that one cannot return to the life that they were originally intended to live without Jesus Christ. After all, He is the one who created that life for us. Fortunately, He is still there waiting, waiting to take us back to that life once we turn to Him and surrender the self-life, our life as a poser, which we have been stuck in for so many years.

Then he said to them all: "Whoever wants to be my disciple must deny themselves and take up their cross daily and follow me." Luke 9:23

Chapter 21

Who Am I Now?

A substantial factor in determining whether we are able to successfully return to the person that we were originally created to be, and leave the poser life behind, is in knowing who we truly are. And not only knowing but truly believing that this is who we are.

For the poser, this can be a challenge, as who and what we are changes quite frequently, adapting to the environment that we are in, as we perceive it to be necessary in order to obtain the love, admiration, and attention that we so desire.

For us to know who and what we truly are requires us to possess a set of core beliefs, which we began to build on in Step 2 of our process. These core beliefs are our foundation, and will essentially determine who we are, what we become, and how we act and react. Therefore, it is imperative that any and all of our core beliefs be based upon the truth and reality. For if they are not, we are once again building a life based upon lies and falsehoods, a life that will never be true or real.

We have also discovered how to build upon these new core beliefs, while eliminating our old beliefs which are flawed and inaccurate. The process of rebuilding these beliefs will take time as we deliberately validate any and all new information that we take in to ensure its truth and credibility.

To help you get started in the process, the remainder of this chapter will highlight just a few of the truths about who you really are. We will also discuss some of the things that tend to hold us back, keeping us in that bondage, which we are most often unaware of. You can take these new truths and engrain them into your core beliefs with confidence as they are trustworthy, they are reality, and have been tested and validated by many sources, including the Bible. Some of these truths may be a bit difficult to fully appreciate at the moment, but that's simply because you don't know who you truly are yet. You are still learning, and relearning. However, this struggle is perfectly normal, as long as you are willing to open yourself up and begin accepting the confirmed truth.

Let us also remember – change is never comfortable, nor should it be.

Agreements

We've touched a bit on the topic of agreements in Chapter 7. Let's now take a deeper look into those agreements which we tend to accommodate, and the impact they have on our lives and who we become.

Agreements are a belief that we align ourselves with. A thought, an idea, a suggestion, an image or observation. And yes, even a perception. When we choose to agree with these notions, we are implying that we perceive them as being the truth and a reality. The fact that they may or may not be true or real has no relevance, as in our mind we have just made them an actuality. Either way, our alignment with them has now made them a part of our reality, and what we believe and see as being true.

Agreements that we make can be either good or bad, having either a positive or negative influence on our lives. They come in all shapes and sizes and can vary greatly in the impact they have from being rather insignificant to completely life altering.

We've already mentioned a few of the negative agreements that we tend to make during our previous discussion on the matter in Chapter 7, but let's highlight them again:

- I am no good and will never amount to anything special.
- I have a crappy life and those are just the cards that I was dealt.
- Bad things happen to me all the time.
- Nothing good ever happens in my life.
- I don't deserve to be loved so it is no surprise that I don't have any friends.
- I am not very good at anything, so why even try.
- I can't rely on other people to be there when I need them.
- Other people only care about themselves. To protect myself from being hurt again I'm going to trust no one.
- I can't let others see the true me – the me that is shameful and embarrassing. And one of my favorites -
- Here we go again!

These are but a few of the lies that we fall into agreement with which hold us back and limit us from realizing our true potential and who we were really created to be. The thoughts, ideas, and images planted into our mind, which are small at first, but quickly grow out of control as we buy into them and accept them as being true. We have also come to realize that this is Satan's plan, to keep us in bondage and prevent us from living the life that was created for us.

So how do we break these negative agreements that we have made so that we are able to move forward and get back on track?

First and foremost, we need to become aware of the agreements which we have made in the past, and then learn to recognize the new ones when they tempt us to buy in.

As for the past agreements that we have made – we need to break those agreements and replace them with the truth. All of these agreements are essentially a contract that we have made with Satan and the kingdom of darkness, stating that we choose to align with what he is telling us. The good news is that contracts can be rescinded or canceled. And that is exactly what we must do with these types of agreements. We must vocally declare to Satan that we are breaking these agreements, while at the same time replacing that lie with the truth that we now fall into agreement with. It is also imperative that we do this out loud, as Satan cannot read our mind or our thoughts.

Here is an example of how we would break an agreement, using the first negative agreement from above:

I renounce the agreement that I have made with the kingdom of darkness that I am no good and will never amount to anything special. I see through this lie and the attempts to keep me in bondage. I choose to live my life in the truth, the truth that I am created in the perfect image of God, and in Christ I am everything and can do anything.

This is just an example, of course. You will obviously input your own agreements which you have made, and you can replace that agreement with whatever truth you would like. Just make sure it actually is the truth.

So, with all of those little voices and thoughts popping into our mind, how are we to know which ones are good and which ones are lies and falsehoods? Not so easy to determine at first. Afterall, Satan is the master of deception, and he is going to make those lies and falsehoods appear to be innocent and real. He will do whatever he can to make us see them as the truth.

The bottom line is this – the truth only comes from the Kingdom of God. Satan, evil spirits and dark forces, and the kingdom of darkness do not and cannot spread the truth. So, when those little thoughts, ideas, or notions pop into your head – ask yourself one simple question: *Is this what my loving Father would say to me?*

When we know who our Father truly is, and who we are in Christ, we should be able to quickly flush out the noise that is constantly trying to keep us in the darkness and in bondage.

Who am I now in Christ?

Yesterday we celebrated Easter. For me, Easter is kind of a big thing. I genuinely understand the significance and importance of what took place two thousand years ago, as well as the ramifications that it has on my life today.

Easter Sunday has a different meaning to many of us. For most it is just one of the few Sundays that we are supposed to attend church, or that we feel obligated to, again, in an attempt to pass ourselves off as being a Christian. Classical poser mannerisms.

For others it is more of a habit or routine that has been handed down to us through our parents or grandparents. It is just something that we do, or that we should do to remain in the good graces of God. As we start our own family and have children, we insist that they too be indoctrinated into this belief and make it mandatory that our families attend church on these major religious holidays. And then, much as the poser does, we run straight back to our everyday lives, outwardly implying that the day has no significance or meaning to it at all.

Then there are those who hold a deeper understanding of what Easter actually signifies. Unfortunately, while they may know what took place on Easter, they still fail to fully comprehend what it means for their life today.

So what is so special about Easter? And why should it have such an impact on our lives today? Let's break it out, with a quick and simple explanation, so that we can all understand.

Easter Sunday is preceded by Good Friday, which begins our explanation. It was the Friday of *Holy Week* and Jesus was being led up to Calvary to be crucified for crimes He did not commit. He would be hung on a wooden cross with spikes driven through his wrists and feet, to be left hanging until He died. Roughly three hours later, Jesus took His last breath.

Jesus was later taken down from the cross and buried in a tomb, which we would be more familiar with today as a cave, and a large stone was rolled in front to cover the entrance. This stone would have weighed roughly three to four thousand pounds and would have taken many men to move into place. Jesus, the one who was supposed to be the Messiah, the New King, dead in a grave. How could this be? His followers and disciples could not understand.

A few days later, Mary Magdalene was going to the tomb. When she arrived, the stone had been rolled away and the tomb was empty. How was this possible? After all, the tomb was being guarded by Roman soldiers to prevent the disciples from stealing Jesus' body and claiming a resurrection. The Roman soldiers had been confronted by an angel, who put the guards to sleep and rolled away the stone.

On the third day, Easter Sunday, Jesus Christ was resurrected from the tomb and brought back to life by the Holy Spirit. Easter Sunday signifies the resurrection of Christ.

But what does all of this mean for us today, and for us who choose to follow Jesus? Let's go back to Good Friday to start with, when Jesus was crucified. His death and His spilled blood are the atonement or sacrifice for our sins. If we are in Christ, all of our sins, past/present/future, have been forgiven and wiped away by the blood of this sacrifice. We are now seen as 'not guilty' in God's eyes. Through His life on earth, and His sacrifice, Jesus conquered sin.

The resurrection on Easter Sunday, Jesus being raised from the dead by the Holy Spirit, is where Jesus conquered death. Without His resurrection, death would still be out fate. Through His resurrection, we are set free from the bondage of sin and death and are promised an eternal life with Christ.

Easter Sunday means that we are totally free! In Christ our freedom has already been purchased and guaranteed. I think this is where most all of us begin to struggle, however. We know that Christ died for our sins, and we even know that He was raised from the dead. What we fail to realize as Christians, however, is twofold:

1) Through His crucifixion, we are no longer sinners. As we are one with Christ, we have defeated sin as well and are no longer controlled by it. Yes, we may still sin on occasion from time to time, but it is not who we are, and it does not define us.

2) Through His resurrection, we have defeated death as well. The death that comes from sin, with an eternal life in Hell. Yes, our bodies will still pass away at some point in time, but we will live forever with Christ. We are free! Completely free from the bondage that sin and death hold us in.

Okay, so we are no longer sinners, and we have been given our freedom. Once again, another misunderstanding that we fail to see the true meaning of. Thanks to the veil of darkness placed over our lives, very few of us are able to fully realize what this means.

What all of this means is that through the death and resurrection of Christ two thousand years ago, our loving Father has made promises and given powers, authority, and freedom to us that we not only fail to recognize but are unwilling to accept and live in as well. All of the work was done long ago through Jesus Christ. All of the promises were made long ago through Jesus Christ and are still readily available to us today. However, for one reason or another, we simply refuse to accept the life and promises that our Father has made for us. We refuse to accept and claim the life, powers, abilities, and freedom that He has made for us through the sacrifice of His only son.

Freedom

Much of our struggle comes from the fact that we really don't know what freedom is. To know and fully appreciate what freedom is, we must also know what bondage or subjection is. The difficulty for much of our current generation is that we live in and have been raised with an attitude of entitlement. In our world, we are king, and we feel that everyone else owes us and is therefore subject to us. With that mentality, along with the lack of teaching on the powers of darkness from the modern-day church, most people today don't ever see themselves as being held in slavery or bondage. And since we are unable to realize that we are being held captive, any offer of freedom has no value to us.

But yet again, we are not supposed to be aware of our enslavement. That is the plan. That is the way it was designed. For as long as we are oblivious, Satan has us right where he wants us and there is little left to be done on his part.

The offer of freedom in Christ is very true and real. The freedom which we receive through Christ is also something that we most often don't accurately perceive.

What actually is this freedom that we supposedly have in Christ? Is it for everyone, and if so, why is it that my life doesn't feel very free.

For many of us that are Christians, we are told, or led to believe, that when we accept Christ as our Savior, we are set free. We're never really told what it is that we are free from, or how this so-called freedom should impact our lives. And with most all of us, since our perception of Jesus and our salvation is flawed to begin with, we perceive that this freedom, along with most all of the other promises that we have inherited, are something that we will obtain once we get to Heaven.

The truth is that ALL of the promises and inheritances that have been given to us through Jesus Christ have been ours for the taking since the day that Christ rose from the grave. A whole 'nother book wouldn't be sufficient to cover everything that we have inherited.

Freedom is just one of the gifts that we have been given through Christ, and it too has been ours for the taking since He defeated death. The problem is that most of us don't claim it. We don't fully believe that it applies to us now, and we also don't fully comprehend what that freedom actually means. There may be a select few that do acknowledge this freedom in Christ, but even then, their understanding of it has been reduced to believing that they are freed from going to hell.

Yes, it is true, our salvation has freed us from spending an eternity in hell. But there is so much more to this freedom that we have been given and that we can live in today, right now!

When we choose to live in Christ, we are set free from the bondage of sin. We are also set free from being owned by Satan. Yes, that's right, Satan. When Christ was crucified on the cross, His blood was the payment for our sins, our freedom, and our souls. Christ purchased us with His very own blood. It is the blood of Christ that set us free, and the blood of Christ which keeps us free. The payment for our freedom was made some two thousand years ago. Our freedom has already been bought and paid for. We just need to step forward and claim that freedom.

So, what is it that we are actually free from? Well, obviously from sin and an eternity in hell. But what about the here and now? How is it that this freedom benefits us in the day-to-day disaster that we call our lives?

If we are able to allow ourselves to actually grab hold of this reality, true freedom in Christ, it will have a major impact on our lives every single day. What we will soon come to realize is that a very large majority of what we fill our lives with, along with what we allow to steer and guide us, is simply meaningless and irrelevant. It is insignificant. It has no importance or value at all.

The vast majority of this rubbish which we allow to overwhelm us was placed there intentionally, by Satan, with the purpose of distracting us, keeping us busy, and keeping us in that bondage by increasing our anger, fear, frustration, desperation, and stress.

We get so wrapped up in the news, social media, current events, and many other worldly matters that we allow each and every one of them to dictate and steer our emotions and our lives. We also become so focused on how others perceive us and what they may think of us that we are willing to change who we are at the drop of a hat just to gain their approval. And while it may be indirectly; these things, and these people, control us. We live our lives every day allowing all of these people and events to dictate who we are and what we do. That my friends, is bondage.

The good news, and the truth, is that we don't have to live there. Allowing any of these things into our lives and our minds is simply a choice. A choice which we have the freedom to make. Satan wants us to accept these things as being 'just the way things are' and make the choice to live with them and in them.

When we choose not to allow these things into our lives we step away from that bondage and into our freedom. When we intentionally decide to not allow anything or anyone other than Jesus Christ have control over who we are and what we become, then we have claimed our freedom.

Once we have made that intentional decision, the accusations, the defamation, the lies, the shame, the guilt; they all fade away as we have chosen to no longer live in them or allow them to control who we are or how we respond. We no longer allow situations or circumstances to fill us with fear or expectations. We no longer allow the comments or feelings of another person to offend us as we are aware that our self-worth is not determined by their approval. Once we make that intentional decision, the vast majority of people and things in this world become insignificant.

And just like everything else in our lives, once something becomes insignificant or unimportant to us, we no longer give it much thought or allow it to have any control over our attitude, emotions, or direction. In a sense, we no longer care about that something.

The freedom is ours for the taking. The only thing holding us back from living in that freedom is a choice. The wholehearted, intentional, fully committed choice to follow and live within Christ.

How long will you wait before you begin to take possession of that which the Lord has given you?   Joshua 18:3

The Truths

We've touched on a few of the negative agreements that tend to hold us back, which once again are intentional and designed to keep us living in bondage. Now let's take a look at what the truths are and then use these truths to replace those lies which we have accepted as our reality.

- God has always been there for us and always will be.

God has never abandoned us or forsaken us and never will. The lie that Satan wants us to believe is that there is no God, or that God has left us to ourselves to figure things out. All books of the Bible undeniably show proof that God has always been pursuing us, desiring us, and wanting us back; regardless of how sinful we may have been. The book of Judges is a perfect example, showing this clearly over and over again. God's people continuously turned away from Him generation after generation only to chase after other gods and their own sinful desires. After years of being overrun and enslaved by other nations, the people would eventually come begging for God to save them. Time and time again, God was always there, wanting them back, and always providing redemption.

- We were created in the image of God, to be perfect in every way.

Yes, each and every one of us was created to be perfect. I know that many of us see something that is far less than perfect when we look in the mirror. We also see much of the same when we look at others. This, however, is only our perception. The perception which has been greatly distorted and flawed. However, it is not the perception that God has of us. We will never be able to see things the way God does. And while it is true that we may have strayed a great distance from that perfect person that we were created to be, that perfect person is still who we were created to be and is still who we can be. It is who we are, if we choose to live in the truth and up to our full potential. And that true person that we were created to be is who God sees when He looks at us.

- In Christ, we are completely free.

Free from the bondage, the lies, and the deceptions which keep us living in a life of fear. In Christ, we no longer have to allow the accusations, the lies, the guilt, or the shame to control us as we now see them for what they really are. We now know that none of it is true, therefore, we no longer have to buy into it or allow any of it to affect us or offend us. We now know that these things have no power over us. The only opinion that matters is that of our Father and Jesus Christ.

- I can give up the life of the poser, and just be myself, as being me is good enough!

In Christ and through Christ, the person that we are and were created to be is more than good enough – no matter what anyone else may think or say. We need to stop trying to be someone or something different only to gain the attentions and praises of other people. We need to start finding our way back to that person that we were created to be and then focus our efforts on gaining the attention of our Father and Jesus Christ. We need to focus on being the best person that we can be, with all of the skills and abilities that each of us has been given. Each and every one of us was made the way that we were, no matter how different or unique that may be, because God has plans for each and every one of us that can only be accomplished by us being our true selves.

Bottom line question – Am I being the best person that I can be, as me, in everything that I do?

- My past does not define who I am.

As we have learned, every one of us has received wounds in our past. We have also learned that it is not so much the wounds themselves which tend to redefine who we are, but more so the way in which we perceive those wounds to have an effect on us. The truth is that these wounds do not define us in any way. They say nothing about who we are or who we should become. The wounds and the ensuing shame are nothing more than lies that are, once again, meant to keep us in bondage and keep us from realizing who we are truly meant to be. We do not have to accept them! We do not have to believe them! And we do not have to live in them!

Many of us struggle to fully accept these truths as being reality for one reason or another. I personally believe this is largely in part due to the fact that most of us don't truly know who our Father is and how much He loves us. It is our perception of who God is and what His true character is that leaves us well short of realizing all of His promises.

Do we not know that we are truly loved by our Father? Loved in a way that is greater than we have ever known or can comprehend. Or is it that we just don't believe it to be true?

A child that knows they are truly loved by their parents unquestionably follows and trusts in their direction and guidance. A child that questions or does not know the love of their parents will always seek to find that love elsewhere. That elsewhere almost never has our best interest at heart.

Do you recall Chapter 2, and the well-known quote from W. Clement Stone – *"We are all a product of our own environment"*? Regardless of whether one claims to be a Christian or not, both the scientific world and The Bible have repeatedly established this statement to be true and accurate, resonating with all people across every generation and society.

If then, we truly are a product of our own environment, wouldn't it behoove us to spend more time in an environment with God and Jesus Christ?

Would it also not be best for the environment that we are in to be our true selves, since being our true self is actually what the world needs? Not another copy of someone else, just us, being our true selves.

"So do not fear, for I am with you; do not be dismayed, for I am your God. I will strengthen you and help you; I will uphold you with my righteous right hand."
Isaiah 41:10

References

<u>Chapter 1:</u>

1 – quote by Oscar Wilde (1854-1900) - The Picture of Dorian Gray - 1891

2 – *Wild At Heart* book - Copyright© 2025 by John Eldredge – Thomas Nelson Publishers

3 – Quote from John Eldredge/Wild at Heart Podcast – WildatHeart.org

4 – *I Don't Have A Clue How To Live This Life* – Copyright© 2025 by Ken Jones

<u>Chapter 2:</u>

1 – quote by Emile M. Cioran (1911-1995)– A Short History of Decay - 1949 Romanian Philosopher and Nihilist

2 – Clance, P., & Imes, S. (1978). The impostor phenomenon in high achieving women: Dynamics and therapeutic intervention. Psychotherapy: Theory, Research & Practice, 15(3), 241–247. https://doi.org/10.1037/h0086006

3 – The Diagnostic and Statistical Manual of Mental Disorders – American Psychiatric Association – International Classification of Diseases

4 – W. Clement Stone (1902-2002) – American businessman and philanthropist.

Chapter 4:

1 – Maslow's Hierarchy of Needs – Wikipedia – https://en.wikipedia.org/wiki/Maslow%27s_hierarchy_of_needs

2 – A Theory of Human Motivation – Abraham Maslow (1908-1970) – Copyright© 2013 Martino Publishing

3 – The Divine Conspiracy – Dallas Willard (1935-2013). Copyright© 1998 by Dallas Willard. HarperCollins Publishers.

4 – Life Together – Dietrich Bonhoeffer (1906-1945) New York; Harper & Row 1954

Chapter 5:

1 – The Bondage Breaker – Dr. Neil T. Anderson. Copyright © 2000 Neil T. Anderson. Published by Monarch Books.

2 – The Handbook for Spiritual Warfare – Dr. Ed Murphy. Copyright©1992, 1996, 2003 by Edward F. Murphy. Published by Thomas Nelson, Inc.

3 – "War." Merriam-Webster.com Dictionary, Merriam-Webster, https://www.merriam-webster.com/dictionary/war. Accessed 13 Jun. 2025.

4 – John Eldredge – Wild at Heart and WildatHeart.org

Chapter 6:

1 – 11 fun facts about your brain – https://www.nm.org/healthbeat/healthy-tips/11-fun-facts-about-your-brain

2 – Closed-eye hallucination – Wikipedia, https://en.wikipedia.org/wiki/Closed-eye_hallucination#

3 – Christopher Butler – Understanding the Eye-Mind Connection – https://www.chrbutler.com/understanding-the-eye-mind-connection#:~:text =What%20these%20studies%20suggest%20is,has%20major%20implications% 20for%20design.

Chapter 7:

1 – *The Anxiety Workbook: A 7-Week Plan to Overcome Anxiety, Stop Worrying, and End Panic* - Arlin Cunic, MA. 2017 by Althea Press

2 – What is shame? – Arlin Cunic, MA. https://www.verywellmind.com/ what-is-shame-5115076#toc-types-of-shame

3 - Narcissist Merriam-Webster.com Dictionary, Merriam-Webster, https:/ /www.merriam-webster.com/dictionary/narcissist. Accessed 15 Jul. 2025.

4 – Condemnation – Vocabulary.com Dictionary, Vocabulary.com, https: //www.vocabulary.com/dictionary/condemnation.

5 – *Never Surrender*   Triumph   1982 Attic Records (Canada), 1983 RCA Records (USA)

Chapter 8:

1- Divide and conquer. Merriam-Webster.com Dictionary, Merriam-Webster, https://www.merriam-webster.com/dictionary/divide%20and%20conqu er. Accessed 19 Jul. 2025.

2- Propensity - Merriam-Webster.com Dictionary, Merriam-Webster, https ://www.merriam-webster.com/dictionary/propensity. Accessed 21 Jul. 2025.

Chapter 9:

1 – Religion – Merriam-Webster.com Dictionary, Merriam-Webster, https:// www.merriam-webster.com/dictionary/religion. Accessed 10 Aug. 2025.

Chapter 11:

1 – Desire – Merriam-Webster.com Dictionary, Merriam-Webster, https://www.merriam-webster.com/dictionary/desire. Accessed 13 Aug. 2025.

2 – Desire – Wikipedia – https://en.wikipedia.org/wiki/Desire#

3 – Desire and Consider: A History – https://www.merriam-webster.com/wordplay/the-history-of-desire-and-consider

4 – C.S. Lewis quote – Joy – Surprised by Joy: The Shape of My Early Life – Copyright© 1955 C.S. Lewis – Harper Collins Publishing

5 – Joy quote – https://www.1517.org/articles/cs-lewis-on-joy#

Chapter 13:

1 – Fortinet – Types of Cyber Attacks – https://www.fortinet.com/resources/cyberglossary/types-of-cyber-attacks

2 – Dallas Willard quote – *The Divine Conspiracy* pg 363 – Copyright© 1988 – HarperCollins Publishers Inc

Chapter 14:

1 – Dallas Willard quote

Chapter 15:

1 – Quote from Freedom In Christ Ministries

2 – William Gurnall (1617-1679) – *The Christian In Complete Armour*

3 – Dallas Willard quote – *The Divine Conspiracy* pg 345 – Copyright© 1988 – HarperCollins Publishers Inc

4 – The Handbook for Spiritual Warfare – Dr. Ed Murphy. Copyright©1992, 1996, 2003 by Edward F. Murphy. Published by Thomas Nelson, Inc.

5 – Eva Krockow, Psychologist – PsychologyToday.com – https://www.psychologytoday.com/us/blog/stretching-theory/201809/how-many-decisions-do-we-make-each-day

6 – *Mere Christianity* – C.S Lewis – Copyright© 1952

7 – *Life Together* – Dietrich Bonhoeffer. Copyright© 2024 – SCM Press

8 – Dallas Willard quote – *The Divine Conspiracy* pg 337 – Copyright© 1988 – HarperCollins Publishers Inc

9 – Confidence – definition – https://dictionary.cambridge.org/us/dictionary/english/confidence

10 – Henri Nouwen quote taken from *The Divine Conspiracy* pg 332 – Dallas Willard Copyright© 1988 – HarperCollins Publishers Inc

Chapter 16:

1 – Dr. Charles Stanley quote – Charles Stanley (1932-2023) – In Touch Ministries

2 – Charles Stanley quote – *Every Day in His Presence* – Copyright© 2014 by Charles F. Stanley – Thomas Nelson Publishers

Chapter 17:

1 – Quote from Albert Einstein

2 – Chariga – https://www.pealim.com/dict/7562-chariga/

Chapter 18:

1 – *The Weight of Glory* – C.S Lewis – Copyright© 1949 by The Macmillan Company New York

Discover the path to your freedom and the real truths. Unlock a wealth of resources by visiting our website at DontHaveAClue.org and begin the journey back to the person that you were created to be. The REAL you returns today!

Enhance your upcoming event by booking Ken Jones as a speaker! For inquiries and scheduling, please visit our website at DontHaveAClue.org. Don't miss the chance to motivate your audience and help them reach their full potential!

Additional books by Ken Jones, including **The Poser** and **I Don't Have A Clue How To Live This Life**, can be found at most outlets, including Amazon.

Join the thousands of others who now have a clue and know the truths. Become part of the movement, reclaim your freedom, and unlock true insight and knowledge today!

www.DontHaveAClue.org

 DontHaveAClue_thebook

 /DontHaveAClue.org

 @AuthorKenJones